GW00722612

WHO BUILT OUR ARCHIVE?

Celebrating 70 years of
The Omnibus Society Library & Archive

Ted Gadsby

The following quotation refers to the enthusiast fraternity typical in the first 50 years of The Omnibus Society (1929-1979) – extracted from the Golden Omnibus, published by the Society, and may give more than a hint as to why our archive exists.

> **66**
>
> *Some of these quieter, solitary ones don't keep their worries to themselves, but write letters, long letters, frequent letters, demanding letters, letters asking questions, letters requesting photographs, timetable information. Letters are answered, and back come more letters. Where does all the knowledge go to – the Archives of course. Much of what is written here applies to any old enthusiast, but we are The Senior Society, preserving for posterity. We must have archives.*

John Edward Dunabin (1916-2002)

*This history is dedicated to all those who have contributed materially
and by personal devotion to build our archive over 70 years*

On the prowl is West Yorkshire Road Car Co. 185, CW 7022, a Leyland Lioness,
ex-Keighley Brothers, shuttling down from the Cow & Calf Hotel, high above
Ilkley. The PLC1 chassis later ended up with a lorry body. WYIS:10302A

WHO BUILT OUR ARCHIVE? was edited by Gavin Booth and published by
The Omnibus Society, 100-102 Sandwell Street, Walsall, WS1 3EB

First published 2012 ISBN 978-1-909091-00-9 © The Omnibus Society 2012
Design by Mark Watkins, Luck Design. Printed by The Lavenham Press Ltd, Lavenham, Suffolk

Celebrating 70 years of the Archive

2012 marks the 70th anniversary of the foundation of the Omnibus Society Central Timetable Collection, which has fully blossomed into its archive. Is this the right time to write its history? In 2011, Barry Le Jeune passed over the mantle of Chairmanship, making us realise how the dreams of our founders have been realised over the time since he first took office. Is it visionary management, the cause of social history, nostalgia, the desire to relate past experiences, generosity in volunteering our resources, technology or just good luck that have played their part? As the author reads through the pages of the Omnibus Society's history, he realises it is all of these. The Archive portrays the generosity of the dedicated, the inspiration of a few and the dogged determination of many to nurture and improve it. Although growing exponentially, to the extent that we must now question where we are going with it, it has not always been a happy growth. Because of lack of funds, giving past rise to accommodation far from the standard we now enjoy, there have been many stops and starts in its progress. This has led to the 'wheel being reinvented' several times – inventories being neither continuous nor handed on. A most notable exception to this lack of continuity has been in tickets, thanks to two stalwarts, – Reg Durrant and Rev Pat Lidgett – in whose safe hands the successive custody of our collection has been since at least 1946, an extraordinary record. Yet as the collection grows, such is the need for quicker access and intelligent retrieval, presenting us with the challenge of using technology to search for the detailed picture. In an age of transparency and immediacy, we need to question our entrenched

LENICE

views on the experience of our gems. Archive material is not just for the researcher – a minority of us carry out learned research – but many of us wish to touch our past, to feast upon that elusive article hidden for 70 years, see the 2d trolleybus ticket, scrutinise a photograph of our school bus in its street environment, study the timetable which showed our progressive journey to see Aunt Jane or delve into the vagaries of joint operation. With an archive gem like ours, must we not share that experience with a wider audience in its search for intelligent history? Enough philosophy – how did it all start?

Ted Gadsby

CHAPTER 1

Sevenoaks to Ladbroke Grove

COLLECTING THINGS
IS THIS HOW IT ALL BEGAN?

Wandering near Chelsea Station, between King's Road and Fulham Road, the very young boy found an isolated hollow area where the wind vortices accumulated a veritable assortment of coloured tickets. Arriving home with a pocketful he set them out on the table, but his mother reprimanded him for handling tickets contaminated by 'all sorts of persons' – and committed them directly to the fire.

So, we guarantee that no such soiled tickets came to the Omnibus Society (OS), but this young mid-1890s six-year old and his brother were about to embark on forming a unique London, Provincial & Foreign transport collection covering an extensive 70-year period (1880-1950). The fruits of this collection are now lodged with the London Transport Museum (See Reinohl, page 52), but the Society benefited from the generous gift of many duplicate tickets. They form much of the oldest part of our archive. So in what sequence were the main sections of our archive first collected?

Collecting tickets certainly dates from the 1880s, or earlier, of which our archive has plenty. Times of horse buses had appeared in local newspapers for decades; horse and steam trams were soon incorporated, but few of these are held by the OS and enquiry at newspaper archives may find results. Urban frequency of electric trams and early motorbuses generally justified only first and last departures of the day for each route, and these began to appear in 'ABCs' produced by newspapers, other printers, and in railway guides. Collectable operator timetables started to appear around 1912, permitting eager acquisition of booklets from around the UK and Ireland.

Perhaps it was in London that the first route and vehicle observations were recorded by enthusiasts prior to the turn of the 20th century. Photographs became the next wave of enthusiast collections, primarily from the late 1920s, but in earnest from 1950 when film again became available.

Paragon two-horse bus, plying from Liverpool Street Station to Effra Road, Brixton. (Sisley 0660)

EMBRYO DAYS

Founder Charles Lee is known to have been writing to operators asking for timetables as early as October 1917 – at the age of 16 – and also hoarded newspaper cuttings (letter from Lee held by the Science Museum refers). He gained timetabling experience as an assistant compiler of the 1920s 'Travel By Road Guide' (TBR). E Melville Upton, a founder member, gained interest in services and tickets during the Great War and afterwards. John Fielder, another founder member, used the TBR Guide at the age of nine in 1923 as he explored early bus services. From its foundation in late November 1929, and under Lee's Chairmanship, the Omnibus Society (OS) membership gained knowledge from learned papers presented at London venues, coupled with visits to witness buses in operation. One of these papers was read on 5 April 1935 by member Cyril Tibbett (see 'Who's who?'), Managing Director of Index Publishers (Dunstable) Ltd, on 'Public Time Tables', dealing with *problems of production of official timetable books for single operators and the general timetables for various localities'*, in which the author's firm has specialised.

Alec Jenson's talk, on 5 March 1937, on road passenger transport in the Black Country was illustrated with lantern slides, historical maps and samples of tickets and photographs. Those attending these two meetings, at least, must have been inspired to collect and copy memorabilia for their own areas of interest. Iolo Watkin, an enthusiastic ticket collector, who exchanged tickets with Reg Durrant, had admired the latter's well-ordered system and decided around 1937 to hand over his examples to incorporate into Durrant's collection, thereby enhancing what became the OS archive. Other individuals took their own photographs and collected timetables and other historical reminders of their interest, but there were few relevant books and even fewer Society records.

In 1938, the 20-year old Leonard Cox put forward his views for extracting information from the 'closed' postal circuits (the means by which recordings and observations were built up) for wider circulation to members in general, thus providing a service previously inaccessible to most provincial members. Council then invited him to join every circuit in order to extract the information likely to be of general interest and report back on his findings. He suggested compiling a list of relevant periodicals. Cox's 'pressure' on Council to open up communications with the membership provided a base for the next step, he, sadly, not living to see its fruition.

> ❝
> ... under Lee's chairmanship, the Omnibus Society membership gained knowledge from learned papers presented at London venues, coupled with visits to witness buses in operation

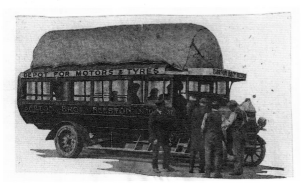

Barton Bros, the pioneering East Midlands bus operator is recalled by this cutting showing a solid-tyred single-decker running on gas, around 1917, during World War 1.

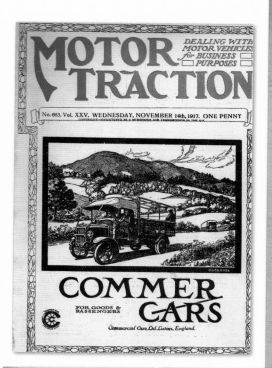

ABOVE LEFT: The Library contains many copies of trade weekly and monthly magazines. This is the cover of a 1917 issue of Motor Traction featuring a War Department Commer troop carrier. Copies of this journal from 1905 are held.

ABOVE: This 1942 Maidstone & District leaflet cover for Summer express services between London and Tenterden includes notes warning of fuel restrictions and restricted areas.

LEFT: A 1934 timetable for Orange Bros services linking Newcastle and Sunderland with London indicates that 'there is no part of the country which may not be reached by its associated services', with connections from Scotland and to south coast resorts indicated on the map.

28 FEBRUARY 1942

So it was that at the AGM on 28 February 1942 (there had been no 1941 AGM), held at 75 Strand, in the dark days of global war, after Charles Lee had read a paper on 'Area Agreements', an Emergency Executive Sub-Committee was elected and empowered to exercise all the ordinary routine powers of Council. A full Council of 14 was elected, two of whom would be killed in the consequences of war, before the year was out. The Council included two new members, John Parke and John Gillham. The 25-year old transport journalist John Parke was promptly appointed assistant secretary, publications. He had recently written to the secretary, Charles Klapper, as follows:

'Dear Mr Klapper, One of the most efficient methods by which the development of bus services in Great Britain may be traced is through timetables, both of operators and those published by printing firms, and it would, I suggest, be of considerable assistance to members of the Omnibus Society if there was a timetable catalogue showing the whereabouts of any particular book. A further possibility for which I would ask your consideration is the formation of a comprehensive collection in the library of the Omnibus Society so that, when the opportunity arrives, it may be housed together with the rest of the collection in the O.S. clubroom. Following the regrettable death of Mr. H. J. Corner, his large collection of timetables passed into my hands and I suggest that his collection, merged with my own, should form the nucleus of an O.S. timetable library. The collection as a whole makes no pretence of being complete and comparatively few of the booklets are dated earlier than 1925 but there must be other members of the Society who can fill the gaps. With their assistance, it should be possible to reach a stage at which it could be said that there existed a reference library, which provided a great part of any information that an Omnibus Society member might require…'

This letter had appeared in a February 1942 Information Sheet, concluding with the concession that few people who are still civilians have time to compile a catalogue. Several objections were raised, alleging that such a collection would be inaccessible to distant members. Access to a Central Collection was difficult, with the drastic restrictions on wartime travel. The facility was set up for timetables to be loaned by post, it being argued that partial dispersal of the collection minimised the danger of loss from air raids – a sign of the times! Cataloguing of timetables to include also those held by members in their own custody, was debated, suggesting that members might provide the odd book to fill a gap in the central collection, without denuding their own! By August an embryo Central Collection, held in John Parke's Sevenoaks residence was recognised, by fusing the collections of the late young John Corner and John Parke himself. This initial help (confirmed in OM:3/43) was attributed to Jack Baker, George Bullock, Bert Chambers, Paul Gomes, Leslie Nicholson and Reg Westgate, among others.

The Secretary's annual report for the 1942 AGM confirmed John Parke as being in charge of the Central Timetable Collection and Edgar Sharpe as photographic registrar.

> ❝
> Access to a Central Collection was difficult, with drastic restrictions on wartime travel, and the facility was set up for timetables to be loaned by post

EARLY POSTWAR DEVELOPMENTS

Postwar developments were being considered, including possible election of a president. At a Papers Committee held in March 1945, Bert Chambers mooted that textbooks should be added to the Library, a Librarian be appointed to Council and that Parke be asked to fill this post. 'After the European War,' he continued, 'premises should be sought for meetings and a room or cupboard might be permanently rented there for the accommodation of the library …

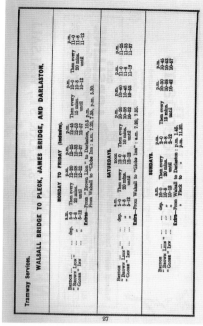

An appropriate item in the Walsall collection – a 1927 Walsall Corporation timetable. This is the cover and a sample page, complete with local advertising on the cover and a pledge from the General Manager & Engineer that complaints or suggestions will receive his 'immediate attention'.

An existing institute or restaurant(!) might provide some sort of facility.' By the end of the war, members had added to the timetable collection and loans by post had been healthy. It had been possible to provide information to government departments, although believed to have been primarily regarding vehicles (Jimmy LaCroix looked after vehicle records).

By September 1946, the first of many reports had been considered by Council recommending a search for rentable premises for meetings and to house the library, particularly after recovery of the finances allowed Edgar Sharpe to reserve funds for the purpose. John Parke, with the collection remaining at his house, considered the matter urgent. Charles Klapper took over as the second OS chairman in January 1947. Reg Durrant had taken charge of ticket matters, being soon co-opted to Council, and in October gave a short paper on 'Tickets: Some aspects of the Society's collection'. John Parke had

additionally become secretary and postal loans were suspended for a year (1947/48) due to coping with the scope of his tasks. At the 1948 AGM Charles Lee, now president, welcomed the assurance of Sir Cyril Hurcomb, chairman of the British Transport Commission, 'of the readiness of the Commission to ensure preservation of the records of transport undertakings'. Would that his word had carried more weight! He also reported on the 'Hancock Relics', referring to framed engravings of the original narrative of Walter Hancock's (1799-1852) pioneer steam road carriages, which had been loaned to the Goodyear Tyre Co in the USA for the duration, and had now been returned to the OS.

The 1949 AGM, held at the Institute of Marine Engineers, found Eric Osborne elected (the third) chairman. Joe Higham was working out a scheme for establishing the photographic register, though little is known of any handover from Edgar Sharpe. One-third of members consulted the timetable collection and generous additions had been made by Jack Baker, George Bullock, George Cookson, Paul Gomes and Charles Lee. By 1950, John Parke was no longer able to house the timetable collection, so they went to the Durrant's, Mrs Durrant becoming curator. The ticket archive had been growing steadily, whilst large collections had been gifted by Bruce Maund and Eric Osborne, with a contribution of tickets coming from Herbert Reinohl. The Durrant's Orpington household really must have been busy!

At the 1952 AGM, held at the Institute of Transport, Graeme Bruce was elected the (fourth) chairman, with William Street as Hon Secretary. Transport books were becoming more available; Charles Klapper and Alan Townsin soon became recognised authors of commercial publications; Ian Allan's 'Buses & Trams' and histories of Red & White and SMT were new entries. Early contacts were made with the Traffic Commissioners, it being important to stock all Notices & Proceedings (N&P), which record applications, refusals, legal wrangles and approvals of the licensing system; binding had started of the 1953 editions.

John Hibbs assumed the post of librarian from April 1954, and pioneered the setting up of OS records, taking in and cataloguing Notices & Proceedings and books, setting rules for the service and founding a Library Committee. His main task consisted of sending out the books to members by post, and recording the same. At the start of 1956, however, he handed over to Peter Gerhold, with Robin Hannay as an assistant librarian (technical) to establish a library of vehicle manufacturers' catalogues. (Convening the Library Committee was intermittent before 1993 and later credit goes to Reg Westgate for its eventual permanence).

Between 1958 and 1960 much of the collected OS material was moved to accommodation on the platform of London Transport's Ladbroke Grove station, seen here in more recent times. These premises were vacated in 1989. *A J Francis*

A DUSTY HOME AT LAST

By 1957, lack of accommodation had become critical. Leslie Nicholson, who looked after the N&Ps, believed that some effort should now be made to gather all the Society's records under one roof. It was proving difficult to spare room in the organisers' homes for the storage of, and access to, this material – Reg Durrant had such a large number of timetables that he feared damage to his house! John Hibbs offered a Bedford bus(!) for storage, if a site could be found, and Derek Giles suggested a notice in the *Omnibus Magazine* (OM) might bring a reply. Eventually, chairman Bruce had heard back from London Transport who had offered accommodation at Ladbroke Grove Station (LG), consisting of three rooms, previously used for refreshments, each 9ftx11ft, alongside the eastbound platform of the former Metropolitan Line. The Chairman and Leslie Nicholson were sent to investigate (5/12/57) and considered it suitable, finding the rent asked to be £20 per annum as from 25 December (yes – Christmas Day!). Once the lease was sorted out the OS could gain possession. Prior cleaning was fundamental. Permits for entry were necessary and M H Ford, who took charge, Jimmy Blair and Douglas Spray were the first holders. Removal of most documents to LG took place from June to August 1958, although some material was left at the homes of Reg Durrant

DECEMBER, 1929

UNDERWOOD
EXPRESS SERVICES, LTD.

MOTOR COACH
TIME TABLE.

WHY NOT? Talk it over with

D. H. KAYE,
EXPERIENCED MOTOR ENGINEER,
50, NAPIER STREET
(ENTRANCE, CORNER OF HARROW STREET),
SHEFFIELD, or Phone 21996.

Lewis

Official
OMNIBUS TIME TABLE

AUGUST, 1933.   Issued Free.

THE LEWIS OMNIBUS COMPANY, LIMITED
Enquiry and Booking Office : 25 MARKET STREET, WATFORD.
Phone : Watford 4488

ABOVE: Two Gilford coaches grace the cover of this 1929 timetable for the express coach services of W T Underwood, which started bus services in the Chesterfield area leading to the creation of the East Midland company.

ABOVE LEFT: An AEC Regent features on the cover of this August 1933 timetable for The Lewis Omnibus Company of Watford. Lewis was taken over by the new London Passenger Transport Board just two months later.

RIGHT: A fine 1932 timetable cover from Blue Bus – the motorbus services of Newcastle Corporation Transport.

BLUE BUS
NEWCASTLE CORPORATION TRANSPORT
TOWN AND COUNTRY SERVICES

1st JULY, 1932,   UNTIL FURTHER NOTICE.
OFFICIAL TIME TABLES.
PRICE ONE PENNY.

ABOVE LEFT: The Birmingham & Midland Motor Omnibus Company grew to be the largest territorial bus company in England outside London. This 1921 timetable cover dates from its earliest days.

ABOVE: An attractive 1932 United Automobile Services timetable cover features a Leyland Tiger used on the company's Newcastle-London services, and contains details of services over a wide area stretching from County Durham to Yorkshire.

LEFT: London-based Rural England Motor Coaches was one of many coaching companies that emerged in the 1920s as motorbuses offered greater speed and comfort. This is a 1928 timetable cover for the Gloucester-London service.

RIGHT: The Tilling Group operator Crosville produced annual Handbooks containing information about the company, which then covered a substantial part of north-west England and North Wales. The 1949 edition featured a Bristol L on the cover.

FAR RIGHT: Coventry suffered badly during World War 2 but Coventry Transport was able to produce this attractive timetable cover in 1942.

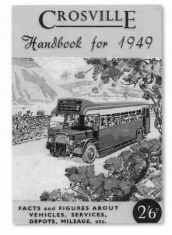

and Peter Gerhold. Leslie Nicholson specifically thanked John Fielder for his help in the removal.

Derek Giles thought that the members should know more about the ticket collection (nothing changes!) and it was agreed that Reg Durrant would write an article and provide an annual display for members. An unsettled period then prevailed. Joe Higham was reluctant to be re-elected as photographic registrar, due to his preferred interest in the London scene, and by February 1958, J P Ramsey had taken over. The OS owned no negatives, the register covering the ownership by members individually. Ramsey's proposal was that members loaned their negatives for printing.

At LG, a period of hard work, but not stability, ensued. How accessible and effective was its location? Ford's curatorship lacked vision and by 1959 John Gillham took over, soon attending on first and third Thursdays; Reg Durrant and Alfred Hendrie were much involved, both with cleaning the premises and providing winter heating. Also lacking focus had been the librarian and photographic registrar – Peter Gerhold and J P Ramsey had both resigned. After much searching, David Simpson, with John Goddard assisting, took the Photographic role. He reported that it was unlikely that the OS could hold large quantities of negatives, but he would act as a clearing house so that members could be advised on which member had photos of any particular vehicle or operator – up to 1925 would be a starting point!

Copies of the more recent National Express Guide are also held.
Chris Warn

1960s – NEW OFFICERS FORGE AHEAD

Reg Durrant was occupied in engendering enthusiasm in operators to preserve their records. He was curator of the Timetable Collection and had moved the remaining stock to LG by late 1960. Briefly, Alfred Hendrie was acting librarian, the post then being taken by Geoffrey Brockington who, by January 1962, had recovered the library held by Peter Gerhold, re-housed it at LG and started listing. Likewise, David Simpson was indexing privately-held photographs. Council reported that the Society's photographic register was at last coming into being.

Late 1961 saw joint consultation with the PSV Circle on applying the Jimmy LaCroix Testimonial Fund towards book purchase. His albums and photographs were listed and these would form the basis of the OS photographic records. Alan Duke said that the scrapbooks were extremely interesting, generally consisting of press cuttings and captions mainly but not entirely of buses, commencing about 1928. Tony Newman worked on these for proper presentation, preservation and accreditation. Alan Duke himself is also remembered as abstracting and providing motor tax records, a service now highly valued.

Some publications were only available on inspection at LG, such was now the anxiety over the danger of loss in the post and by possessiveness, a fear justified by the way the system failed to retrieve all loaned material.

Founder member (no.4) E Melville Upton died accidentally in December 1962. He had been a prolific traveller and timetable collector, and bequeathed his papers, records and tickets, but there was not enough space at LG. His excursion & tours leaflets were still not sorted 40 years later! Again, material became stored in private residences, this time at the homes of Charles Lee and Paul Gomes, whilst Derek Giles was, even at this time, housing many leaflets for the OS. Bill Lambden, who became the fifth chairman in March 1963, soon received communication from the British Library (BL) asking for details of the OS Library – and its first recognition that the OS Timetable Library might be unique.

Bedwas & Machen UDC was one of the smallest British municipal bus fleets. This is a 1964 AEC Regent V with lowbridge Massey bodywork.
Photo by K Smallman © OS SMLLMN5-122

On 1 January 1964, Brian Walter became curator of the Timetable Collection, but with Reg Durrant remaining in overall control until 1967. In April 1966 John Parke became our sixth chairman, and a collection of horse bus tickets was received from Mr Baker of LT. David Simpson struggled with the heavy load of the photographic register and indexing photos in technical journals, so Rev Eric Ogden agreed to take over the Scottish, Northern and North Western & Yorkshire registers. In December 1967 a curator was sought for the Overseas Timetable collection – not now held by the OS, any such material coming in is handed to Buses Worldwide.

> Some publications were only available on inspection at LG, such was now the anxiety over the danger of loss in the post and by possessiveness

UNDERGROUND CONSOLIDATION

During the whole of 1970 the library had suffered disruption at Ladbroke Grove, when the entire stock had to be moved in one weekend into temporary and inaccessible storage in nearby Shepherd's Bush. This was followed by a second upheaval for redecoration.

John Smith entered the scene by 1971, as librarian & archivist, and an article on the library appeared in OM267 providing a full description of the extent of the Library. Material was still loaned out by post, but the unheated LG was open for personal visits, by arrangement, on Wednesday evenings, when advice could be given to would-be researchers.

Brian Walter remained as the timetable collection curator. Reg Durrant continued to exercise care of tickets – a large donation by H G Baker had necessitated 12 more binders, bringing the total to over 50; he also acted as publications officer!

The archive collection was referred to as being built up over many years from items

JONES'
Omnibus Services Ltd.

WARM TURN, ABERBEEG, MON.
Telephone: ABERBEEG 376/377

LUXURY COACH TOURS
and
BUS SERVICE TIMETABLES

6 d.

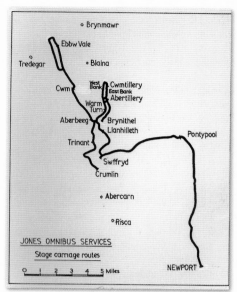

JONES OMNIBUS SERVICES
Stage carriage routes

0 1 2 3 4 5 Miles

A timetable cover and service map for the South Wales independent operator, Jones of Aberbeeg. Jones sold out to the new National Bus Company in 1969.

GREEN BUS
SERVICE

TIME TABLES

Commencing
SEPTEMBER, 1982

5p.

THE GARAGE, LANDYWOOD, GREAT WYRLEY
Telephone: Cheslyn Hay 414141

A 1982 timetable for Green Bus Service of Great Wyrley, Staffordshire.

Service 475

CANNOCK - PENKRIDGE - SHIFNAL - TELFORD
For Shopping Centre, Carrefour Hypermarket, Sainsburys, etc.

THURSDAY ONLY

	am								pm	
CANNOCK (Bus Station)	dep	9 50							1 30	
White Lion		9 53							1 40	
Huntington		9 56							1 41	
Wolgarston		10 02							1 54	
Rockhouse Estate		10 06							1 59	
PENKRIDGE (Crown Bridge)		10 09							2 01	
Gailey		10 15							2 07	
Deansfield Estate		10 21							2 13	
BREWOOD (Market Place)		10 30							2 23	
Kiddemore Green		10 32							2 25	
Bishops Wood		10 38							2 31	
Tong Norton (Cross Roads)		10 41							2 34	
Shifnal (Union Inn)		10 48							2 34	
TELFORD (Town Centre)	arr	10 58							2 37	

WHEATON ASTON - SHIFNAL - TELFORD   Connecting Service

THURSDAY ONLY

	am								pm	
LAPLEY (Vaughan Arms)	dep	10 10							1 30	
The Rookery		10 13							1 40	
Wheaton Aston		10 16							1 54	
Bishops Wood		10 34							1 59	
Shifnal (Union Inn)		10 48							2 04	
TELFORD (Town Centre)	arr	10 58							2 07	

donated by members, and there were familiar messages about not allowing your precious transport material to be tipped out, but transferred to the Library! The full collection would be familiar to present day users. It already consisted of books (with many tramway histories), including fleet books, Society publications, periodicals, Notices & Proceedings and timetables. Indexing of minor operators' leaflets, with cross-referencing of owner/s' and their trading fleet names had been dedicatedly accomplished. The timetables filled more than one room of shelving – 'quite a feast for the enthusiast's eyes'. At this time, a small stock of popular publications was made available at the London meetings.

1970 had seen the retirement of Photographic Registrars, Rev Eric Ogden (north) and David Simpson (south). In March 1973, Arnold Mason took the combined post and wished to extend the register to include photographs available from members' collections. However, he failed to substantiate the posting and the register ceased by default.

In 1973 Tom McLachlan became the seventh member to take the chair of the OS. Membership was 'bubbling', having exceeded the 1,000 mark, but he encountered exacerbating space problems at LG. A suggestion was made to move the Library to the University of Surrey in Guildford, 'incorporating it with that of the Transport Trust.' This was later dismissed on the grounds of geographical location(!), but close liaison was maintained with the Transport Trust of which John Parke had become Secretary.

Although an additional room at LG had become available in 1975, by late 1976 the Library was re-housed in adjacent rooms, consequent upon London Transport (LT) reconstruction to improve their staff rooms, this dislocation necessitated much rebuilding of storage racks, and in 1977 there was only limited library service.

A Library Sub-Committee had been in existence for some years and soon got embroiled in an issue that consumed Council for over a decade – amalgamation of archive material with the PSV Circle, as well as future policy regarding joint publications and other matters of mutual interest. The proposal was for a Joint Memorial (to Jimmy LaCroix) Library – at LG – with funds from his testimonial for book purchases, supplemented by a James Price bequest. This was approved by March 1976, under Tom Smith's supervision, and the Memorial Library (some 400 titles) was highly successful, funds having been set aside for increasing the 'unique collection'. (*Stock in 2011 is over 7,000 books but sadly this priceless collection today is now rarely consulted – perhaps the sheer quantity of publications has submerged its value*).

Lewis Norris appealed to members to fill gaps in the LT area timetable collection of 1936-1971. We stocked 5,000 of the 7,000 issued. This appeal gives some clue as to how the library has built up such near-complete runs of timetables with members help, both in the metropolitan and provincial fields.

COUNCIL NEEDS TO MANAGE!

John King, in May 1974, reviewed the status of the collection. He criticised Council for concentrating on policy at the expense of administration and cited its ignorance that N&Ps were being received officially, hence not ensuring their maintenance for posterity. In late 1975, he further reported the likelihood of having to vacate LG shortly, adding that conditions there were not conducive to conserving manuscripts. Secretary, Marcus Gaywood and treasurer, Terry Dendy were to investigate a list of LT properties available for hire. Some re-allocation of rooms at LG helped and surplus timetables were offered to members to provide space. Opening hours at this time (1979) were Wednesdays 18.00 to 20.00hrs. Thoughts were also given on procedures to be followed on how to cope with the material bequeathed to the OS.

In July 1980 further duplicate tickets from the Reinohl Collection were taken in. Tom Smith, memorial library curator, retired to Lincolnshire in April 1980 and Chris Goodwyn took his place, until he resigned on removal to Suffolk in September 1981. Brian Walter then added the duties of Memorial Library to his

McKindless Group

Timetable Booklet

McKindless Group
Serving the Public

McKindless was one of the Scottish independent operators that emerged following the deregulation of local bus services in 1986. This booklet shows a DAF/Optare Delta bus. It had grown to over 100 vehicles when it ceased trading in 2010.

timetable portfolio from January 1982.

In 1981, John Fielder became the eighth OS chairman and John Parke was elevated to president; total membership peaked at 1,089, but minds were pre-occupied with lack of space in the four rooms then rented at LG.

Malcolm Papes, a new member, had written on his ideas for collating photos and negatives. In March 1982 he assumed the post of photographic registrar, from the interim Stan Denton and Tom Dethridge.

On tickets, Reg Durrant reported that the Rev Patrick Lidgett would be his successor 'when the time came', and would, as he had done, merge his own collection with that of the OS, holding the combined collection for as long as he may wish and eventually choosing his own successor.

It was 1984 and astute members were penning ideas for developing facilities. Dave Bubier thought that the Library should be re-located into more suitable accommodation (Chepstow was mentioned) and that micro-filming should be started, Frank Simpson had visited LG and urged the preservation of original and more valuable items in secure premises with copies made available for reference purposes. John Cockshott (1986) expressed concern that PSV Circle members had no access to what was a joint Memorial Library. He also sought clarification that the Memorial Library was to contain only books bought from the legacies and the joint funds of the OS and PSVC. This had conflicted with a Council minute of May 1975, and an attempted summary by Geoff Morant in June 1986 failed to solve the issue. The Joint Memorial Library sub-committee in 1987 consisted of John Cockshott, David Gray, Derek Roy, John Smith, Brian Walter and Reg Westgate.

John Fielder's term as chairman was short-lived (of necessity, Alan Mills was a busy deputy). Barry Le Jeune started his long term as the ninth Chairman of the OS, in May 1984, with a Council meeting returning to the famous address, 55 Broadway, London SW1. Reg Westgate and Terry Dendy continued in the supporting secretary and treasurer roles. Before long, ideas for improvement were being considered but, with multiple options and unsettling distractions, it proved to be another decade before accommodation and management were settled. Clearly, further occupation at Ladbroke Grove would be short-lived, as Derek Roy, in-between listing the Memorial Library, had to tackle the site engineer on building work which was disrupting our service. In the meantime, an appeal for the return of a number of loaned items for audit was placed – valuable copies of *Modern Transport*, amongst many items, were in this category.

> **"**
> Before long, ideas for improvement were being considered but, with multiple options and unsettling distractions, it proved to be another decade before accommodation and management were settled.

WHITHER THE LIBRARY?
FACING EVICTION

January 1985 found Alan Mills suggesting that the OS consider the *acquisition* of a building in the West Midlands for library accommodation. This foresight took 22 years to come to fruition! John Smith and Brian Walter were consulted over space and 500sq ft was considered necessary

Amongst the varied locations considered suitable for future housing of the archive was 'Kithead', in Droitwich, which the PSV Circle was establishing as a printing and storage facility; prolonged negotiations included the unlikely scenario of the OS taking shares in the venture. Further negotiations ensued which the Council inclined to accept, but deferred a decision.

More optimistically, in discussion with the Transport Trust, an arrangement with Brunel University was given serious thought, a joint meeting being held in February 1987. Access would be available to the general public as well as to OS members, but after Brunel stated they would take only books, not timetables, and demanding a contribution of £2,000, the idea was dropped.

The chairman had written to the British Library seeking advice on financial assistance with archive storage; subsequent response was favourable only in providing funds for binding of further N&Ps and some journals. He also sent a letter to all OS members asking for donations to a fund to improve archive storage. Tony Francis drafted a circular regulating the receipt of material, but the OS 'missed a trick' with regard to the disposal of archives from ex-BMMO Carlyle Works – they ended up with the Birmingham and Midland Motor Omnibus Trust and Birmingham Transport Historical Group! More luckily, Pat Lidgett rescued John King's valuable ticket collection.

Tony Newman resurrected the prospect of organising sales of surplus material for 'younger members' and, in 1988, Alan Mills presented far-sighted thoughts on 'Surplus or Unwanted Bus & Tram material'. This resulted in a paper in January 1989 on an 'OSMART' scheme,

AA Motor Services was one of the famous Ayrshire co-operative bus operators. This is a 1986 Leyland Lynx, part of the Dodds of Troon contribution, at AA's Ayr bus station.
Photo by Pat Sparrow © OS PSprrw 0509

a radical marketing idea subsequently founded and managed by Derek Broadhurst and which was to have a significant mark on the activities of the archive.

The PSV Circle paid up to date for their contribution to the Joint Memorial Library, but the future of the arrangement was 'fraught'.

Further discussions with Kithead resulted in a loan of £1,000 being made by the OS for a building extension and racking, (repaid three years later), and it became urgent to identify what material would be housed there. Members were asked to identify any material rightly owned by the OS; coincidentally a complete audit of LG material was carried out.

The bulk of material was held at LG in the custody of Brian Walter (Memorial Library and Timetable Collection), and John Smith (Society Archives, N&Ps, journals, other publications).

Material not held at LG included Ticket Collection (Reg Durrant/Pat Lidgett); (some) overseas material (Geoff Morant); Minute books (Marcus Gaywood); Photographic archive (Malcolm Papes); press cuttings (Chris Taylor); and *Modern Transport* (Terry Dendy).

In January 1989, although no formal notice to evacuate Ladbroke Grove had been received (it was served on 1/3/89), the chairman led plans for just this. Clearance commenced straightaway with a deadline of 30 June 1989 largely achieved. John Smith expressed his thanks for the task to John Hart, Derek Roy and Brian Walter; Derek Persson, Dave Bubier, Julian Bowden Green (of London Omnibus Traction Society) and Ted Shepherd also played a part.

So ended a major chapter in this history.

CHAPTER 2

Coalbrookdale and Acton

DISPERSAL AND LOOKING NORTHWARDS

The dispersal of the Ladbroke Grove contents was to locations of short holding. Peter Nicholls offered temporary use of a basement in Station Road, Anerley, where provincial timetable books were sent; much of the London collection went to John Smith's residence in Brookman's Park; the Memorial Library books to Brian Walter's house in Hounslow, while independents leaflets ended up with Derek Roy in Islington and West Country timetables with John Crowhurst in St Albans. London Underground Signal Overhaul Shop Stores at Lillie Bridge found accommodation (thanks to Barry Wilkinson) for further leaflets, newspapers and journals and other material. LT magazines were secured at Barry's home.

Throughout 1989, a new environmentally-safe home was sought for the OS library, through appeals and personal contacts, as concern was being expressed over the deterioration of printed paper. Sites as far apart as Crich Tramway Museum and the Science Museum annex at Wroughton (to allow vacation of Anerley) and even at 55 Broadway had been put forward, but officers expressed their concern over access rights and soon ruled them out. British Rail Property in Bristol and even a redundant ecclesiastical edifice or abandoned rural telephone exchange were mentioned! Room at London Regional Transport's Baker Street was mooted and shortly taken up, albeit with some delay; the room was not the one negotiated by the chairman, and stocking had to be six boxes high, rendering access cumbersome. Although this would not answer

the fragmentation of the collections it allowed the final clearance of LG through the take of second copies, some annuals and joint PSV publications. Shelves and cupboards, however, needed further temporary storage at LG.

By 1991, OSMART was fully active, including providing funds for binding copies of OM, and for setting up the basis under which it would regulate transfers to or from the Archive. By 1992, there was a threat to the continued use of Lillie Bridge, and concern about access. At this juncture, the chairman heard from Nick Earl, the PSVC Chairman, saying the Circle were relinquishing their interest in the Joint Memorial Library, and the first mention of housing at the LT Museum (LTM) cropped up.

It was noted that the Transport Trust's Library was being transferred from Brunel University to Coalbrookdale at the Ironbridge Gorge Museum Trust (IGMT), in the 'Valley of Invention', and it was suggested that material might be housed there. In November 1992,

Catalogued and boxed tickets in the OS collection.

... a new environmentally-safe home was sought for the OS library, through appeals and personal contacts, as concern was being expressed over the deterioration of printed paper.

The research area at Coalbrookdale in spring 2007 and bound copies of Notices & Proceedings. *Ted Gadsby*

Brian Chappell outlined the position, explaining the adequacy of storage and security, and rental of £150/annum for five years. Tony Francis reported that space was at least twice that of LG. A letter from John Powell, the Librarian & Information Officer, explained opening times and access facilities and that post could be dealt with. (*John Powell and assistant Joanne still help us to this day to gain access, maintain the environment and ensure security of our belongings*). No Midland member had come forward at the branch AGM to form a Library Team, so alternative arrangements would be needed to sort the material. Council confirmed

its intention to move the prime library to Coalbrookdale, whilst housing second copies and London material in the capital – for the time being at least. An agreement was reached with IGMT and in January 1993, it was announced that part of a room would be available. Through the Routemaster Heritage Trust (RHT), courtesy Colin Curtis, accommodation was obtained at Twickenham (on becoming a Friend of the Trust). Preparatory work started in February 1993 but, on John Smith's resignation, John Hart completed the racking and some items from Lillie Bridge to be housed there on its closure on 28 March 1993.

THE VALLEY OF INVENTION

This was also the date that Coalbrookdale received its first material, and whilst some came from Lillie Bridge, the valued first copy provincial timetables were rescued from the house at Anerley (damp and potentially liable to business rates). Sale of surplus timetables funded some racking that was erected. Alan Mills, Derek Broadhurst, Dave Bubier and some Midland members agreed to sort and manage the collection. Checking the inventory and stacking shelves started in June.

J Mervyn Pugh (centre) opening Coalbrookdale Library on 6th May 1994, with Barry Le Jeune (left) and Brian Chappell looking on.

Council in April considered the future in depth, especially the post of Librarian following John Smith's resignation and the uncertainty of Brian Walter's position. It was decided that there should be a London Curator, which was conferred on John Hart; Alan Mills took on the role of provincial curator, with Derek Roy acting as co-ordinator.

An unsuccessful grant application was made to the Wolfson Foundation, but the Rural Development Commission provided funds for shelving, and the British Library (BL) funds for bookbinding.

A significant move occurred in July, still 1993, as the Rev Patrick Lidgett had received the main ticket collection from Reg Durrant, who was thanked for his many decades as its curator, dating back to 1946. Sadly, Reg died in the following year.

At this time, Twickenham took in bundles of schedules from Reg Westgate, London material held by John Smith, West Country material from John Crowhurst, and boxes of overseas material from Geoff Morant (magazines were destined for

Rev Pat Lidgett at work on the OS ticket collection.

Buses Worldwide). Not good however, was that Twickenham had been flooded, putting items at risk.

A second vanload to Coalbrookdale later that year found the Memorial Library cleared from Brian Walter's and independent leaflets from Derek Roy's houses. On 4 February 1994, Coalbrookdale opened to members. Alan Mills reported that Coalbrookdale had opened on four Fridays with good visitor attendance. Sadly, in May came the news of the death on 27 April 1994 of John F Parke, founder of the Library timetable collection. Only nine days later, 6 May 1994, Coalbrookdale was officially opened by the previous year's OS President, Traffic Commissioner Mervyn Pugh, who unveiled a plaque, decreeing: 'THE OMNIBUS SOCIETY JOHN PARKE MEMORIAL LIBRARY'.

A Library & Archive Sub-Committee (L&ASC) was revived to determine operational policy, disposal/storage, acquisitions, and overseas material. The committee comprised: Derek Roy, John Hart, Derek Broadhurst, Dave Bubier, Alan Mills and Reg Westgate, first meeting at Dr Johnson House in Birmingham on 27 November 1993. Coalbrookdale would open on Fridays from February 1994, for research only, with no loans allowed. A decision on retention of the overseas collection was still awaited. Vigorous attempts were made to recover many missing items. Maidstone & District timetables were only recovered after furtive detective work by Dave Bubier tracked down an errant ex-member who had escaped to the south coast! One member was known to have retained timetables for 25 years! These and many other examples showed up how lax some members' consciences had become and helped to determine future cessation of the postal loan service.

TWICKERS, BAKERS AND NORBERS

From September, Coalbrookdale was staffed by Midland volunteers on the first and third Wednesdays. An interesting aside was that the OS vainly offered to look after the Transport Trust archive that shared the room – no-one else was!

Twickenham had briefly opened to members, but notice to quit by the end of May was received after the failure of the RHT to retain it – concurrently with the necessity to leave Baker Street by 7 August. This is where London Regional Transport's Norbiton Garage came into use, albeit for only eight months, and both Twickenham and Baker Street were cleared. Norbiton conditions were better and there was more space.

The Library & Archive Fund was re-established, prompting the opportunity to finance micro-fiching of rare material and more shelving. Frank Simpson, guru at notating historical data on independents, set about sorting and listing their leaflets. An article in *Classic Bus* on the establishment of an industry-wide bus photography archive prompted Alan Mills to reveal the OS potential.

Two more van loads reached Coalbrookdale; in September all Baker St. holdings and in November racking and provincial second copies from Norbiton – all taken to out-storage in the nearby Wesleyan Chapel. Our days at Norbiton were numbered, the site being cleared on 8 January 1995 of all remaining material,

mostly being of London subjects, this being carried north to the dark, dusty chapel. At this juncture it was admitted that the main room at Coalbrookdale was nearly full – a sentiment which typified the state there for another 12 years – and Dave Bubier was looking for further Midlands storage ideas, including the siting of Portakabins, which could have held seconds and/or OSMART material!

Taking stock, Coalbrookdale had been set up with good access for non-London material, but it was still the intention to 'unlock' the London stuff held in the chapel, and allow members access to it. What better place than in the capital itself!

Meanwhile, OSMART had the means to acquire material, both directly and by donation, to recover all previously-held stock and to expand its outlets. Two branches had lent OSMART money to develop its aims.

Collections from Leicester University arrived, along with the bequests of Jack Vincent, M Nash, Peter Nugent, David Loxley and Des Thorne. The valued Alfred W Monk National Collection was offered to the OS on conditional loan, the principles of which were agreed between Alan Mills and Roger Monk (son of Alfred – 1/97).

In late 1995, the BL approved a grant of £5,000, which the OS would match, for micro-filming timetables and this was carried out in 1997/98, covering major operator timetables up to 1930 and independent leaflets up to 1939. John Bennett assisted with storage and a system for copying of prints.

There was serious concern about the papers of the late founder, Charles Lee, who had died leaving his estate to The Church of England Children's Society. Peter Bancroft and Derek Giles were cataloguing OS material which had gone to the Science Museum and determining future actions.

LT MUSEUM TO THE RESCUE

Search for London-accessible accommodation was being pursued. Space at Ealing Common Depot was considered, enough for the London Collection and research, but not the provincial seconds – and lottery funding would be needed. However, in May 1998 it was confirmed that space would become available to house the OS London Collection at Acton Town Museum Depot when the LT Museum moved there in April 1999. Definition of 'London' was needed following the break-up and sale of London Country Bus Services at deregulation; it was deemed that successor companies and their counties would be treated as 'provincial' and be held at Coalbrookdale, along with London books in the Memorial Library, ensuring its entity. By late 1998, Jonathan Riddell, assistant curator of the LTM, visited Coalbrookdale to see the extent of the London Collection, largely agreeing to making accessible space available at Acton. Following agreement, in October 1999, the OS took possession. Jonathan Riddell assisted John Hart to bring the London material from Coalbrookdale to Acton, storing it on pallets for a few weeks, until the 13 cabinets were assembled. A full stock check took place, revealing some incompleteness. 27 January 2000 was the first day that Acton was open for research.

Some overseas material was still held and, due to space limitation, it was agreed that only material relating to British-owned overseas undertakings would be retained, which Derek Roy would house. Soon afterwards, the collection went to Buses Worldwide.

Alan Cross had managed the photographic printing service since c1993 (as he still does) – negatives firstly pass to him to produce prints. At this time, the John Cull collection was held in the Chapel, with Alan Cross temporarily responsible for the Charles Klapper and other photographic gems.

Through Gavin Booth's help, space was found in the marquee at Showbus 1999 used by *Classic Bus* for OSMART to erect a stall; this was repeated for a number of years, proving of benefit to OSMART's income stream. The author and Wilf Dodds were co-opted on to the sub-committee in 1998/99.

A list of the London material held at Acton was copied onto the LT Museum database, in order to aid common interests. Health & Safety determined that material could not be stacked on the floor, and further cabinets were needed.

Debate on the OS-owned 'Smithies List' (operators recorded up to 1963) was an issue in the 1990s. Arthur Staddon edited it into

The working and computer area at Coalbrookdale in 2007, with small operator files in the background. *Ted Gadsby*

counties, with the object of developing an OS database compatible with that of the PSV Circle (which only *started* from 1959). By 2001, print-outs of the 'Master List of Operators', by county (England & Wales), though not yet complete, were available. Chris Warn demonstrated how, by taking Shropshire as an example, a credible database could be formed. A spreadsheet for Scotland was later produced by Richard Gadsby (P10). From time to time at dates unrecorded, tickets were taken in from very early sources. John Shelborne (of the Transport Ticket Society) had earlier come across an elderly gentleman who had 'hung on' to a range of mint tickets from 1881, some of which were donated to the OS. Tickets from the London horse bus era, having been bequeathed to the LCC Tramways Trust, also found a selection donated to the OS. In a further case, David Jones, of the LCC TT, had found an exercise book containing south-east London and other tickets all dating from 1896, including the ubiquitous London, Camberwell & Dulwich Tramway, which only issued tickets for a short period. Tickets taken in were funded over a period by Pat Lidgett himself. There were generous donations by John King, Stewart Williams and Graham Page, not otherwise recorded.

> ❝
> Some overseas material was still held and, due to space limitation, it was agreed that only material relating to British-owned overseas undertakings would be retained

BUSY ON ALL FRONTS

To broaden horizons, a delegation attended the Roads & Road Transport Conference (as it was) on the subject 'The preservation and disposal of personal collections' which helped our policy in dealing with bequests and defining intake policy. Practices were compared with the National Tramway Museum at Crich. The Library produced a strategy in line with the OS Ten-Year Plan (2003-2012), to help focus on a business-like approach to our aims and development. There was no affordable telephone line at Coalbrookdale, so in those modem-limiting days it was not possible to gain internet access. A computer system was installed in 2002, thanks to Mike Stephens' generosity.

Further bays at Coalbrookdale were offered by our landlord John Powell, and these were soon taken up. N&Ps were given a corner and it was decided that space-eating PSV Circle News Sheets would no longer be held. Peter Tulloch rescued a micro-fiche reader from a Burton library but, regrettably, this technology has been overtaken by digitisation. The facility remains, however, allowing security for the originals.

Regular Coalbrookdale teams at this time were Derek Broadhurst, Wilf Dodds and Ron

Thomas (Tuesdays) and Alan Mills, Peter Tulloch and the author (Wednesdays), with John Hart, Dilwyn Rees, John Crowhurst and Tony Wright at Acton, plus help from David Ruddom. Advancing technology rendered N&Ps to be obtainable from the internet with Dave Sturrrock, and later Andrew Tyldesley, volunteering to download these.

May 2003 found LTM requesting us to move all cabinets to a mezzanine location, still within Acton Depot Museum, a move frustrated by its later refurbishment at Covent Garden; 10 volunteers helped. The 'Standard Box' came into use at Acton in 2005.

At Coalbrookdale, occupation of the nearby Abraham Darby Coach House was considered. (*Whilst others took up this accommodation, in 2011 it is in our use holding the massive collection moved from Derek Giles' Westcliff-on-Sea bungalow*). It was realised that a move round of furniture at Coalbrookdale would allow better working, to cure a serious clash in people-movements. The Transport Trust occupied two of the eight shelving units, which could not be 'invaded', but occupation of the 'shelf-end spaces', although only 66sq ft was possible. With their agreement, our minor operator filing cabinets were moved into this area, freeing up space for the computer and allowing segregation of the visiting researchers from the work of the staff. The June 2004 Council was held there; Alan Mills described the 'first ten years' and showed members the cramped, but improved, layout of the facility. OSMART took a lease on a local shop in Llanrhaeadr-Ym-Mochnant, allowing more space at the Chapel.

> ❝
> There was no affordable telephone line at Coalbrookdale, so in those modem-limiting days it was not possible to gain internet access.

ABOVE: The OS Photographic collection contains many fine inter-war images, like this London Transport former Tilling AEC Regent ST type.
© OS 26/213

RIGHT: Bus photographs taken during World War 2 are rare; this is a London Transport STL type AEC Regent at Victoria Station.
© OS 26/232

BELOW: The OS photographic collection covers the whole of the UK. This former London Transport STL type AEC Regent is seen after sale to Dundee Corporation, in the company of a 1921 Hurst Nelson-built tram.
OS collection Norr 141

Alan Oxley, the OS photo archivist. A corner of the OS Photographic Collection at Long Eaton.

FULL AGAIN – WHERE NEXT?

2004 found Alan Cross wishing to terminate the black & white print service ['by 2006' – but still soldiers on in 2011] – and David Packer offered a conventional black-and-white service. Tony Francis produced a Business Plan to improve the availability of images to members, and to motivate those considering bequeathing photographs that they would be readily accessible. During 2005, Gerald Truran left us his photographs and a separate bequest of £5,000 was made to 'establish a Photographic Archive'. So, Council decided to bring together all photographs and negatives that had been donated to the Society. Peter Tulloch was appointed photographic registrar and put forward his ideas, renting a small storage unit in Derby, but soon had to resign for business reasons. In February 2006, Alan Oxley was appointed, with the photographic archive moving into larger premises at New Tythe Street, Long Eaton. Since that time even a further change of room is proving to be too small and a major shift into another part of the building is being considered. Importantly, the plan to sell photographs on the website was born.

The effects of Ernest Fulton and John Latimer were received. The late Reg Westgate's extensive records had been moved from Nottingham to Acton and Coalbrookdale, whilst in March 2006, the large Swindon Corporation Transport legacy was taken in.

Concern was expressed over impending dispersal of the Science Museum material, especially with the lodging there of certain of Charles Lee's papers, some of which were, rightly, OS property. Derek Giles had continued his vigil of sifting through material for copying, where appropriate.

A Society questionnaire, managed by the library team, revealed only a few members prepared to assist in our work.

Accommodation at Coalbrookdale for the provincial archive had become critical. Certain alternatives were considered, namely, to expand into space rented by the Transport Trust with some agreement as to *their* re-location; relocate the Memorial Library somewhere else, or discuss with the Ironbridge Gorge Museum Trust (IGMT) the renting of either floor of the chapel on its planned refurbishment. Joining a fellow enthusiast organisation was considered, such as at Crich, jointly with the PSV Circle, Coventry Transport Museum or Oxford Bus Museum – it all depended on funding. Even under railway arches in Burton-on-Trent was mentioned! In late 2005, rentals in Telford and Derby were examined as a benchmark before, in March and

August 2006, discussions were held with Karen Armstrong of IGMT. The OS was represented by Tony Francis, Derek Broadhurst and Alan Mills. Terms were discussed on a commercial rental for the lower floor of the chapel, once the occupying ironfounder was evacuated and the place renovated. OS had to face up to how to fund an annual rental of nearly £6,000 and other charges. Funding would necessitate a Members Appeal, with outright purchase of a property being considered as the ultimate goal.

> **"**
> OS had to face up to how to fund an annual rental of nearly £6,000 and other charges.

STAYING IN COALBROOKDALE?

In August 2006, an appeal letter was sent to members by the Chairman, setting out the need for funds and specifically mentioning premises at Coalbrookdale. The Appeal principle was backed by Oliver Howarth writing succinctly in OM469 challenging members to be stirred by the vision of a permanent archive. A northern member suggested Walsall or Wolverhampton as being a more convenient location for access to members and staff. It was clear that Coalbrookdale should not be the long-term location of an accessible archive, particularly if, in the future, the library was to attract more custom.

It was not considered that arrangements with IGMT would be sustainable in the longer term. The best course of action would be to seek a short lease (5+ years) at the Chapel, whilst searching for more accessible long-term premises, eg near a railway station. The L&ASC specified the ideal size and location for the non-London material. Cosford was considered a target area – minimising the distance travelled by current volunteers and adjacent to a suitable railway station on the Wolverhampton-Telford Line. An area of around 2,000sq ft was considered the minimum, costing in the region of £200,000 and with annual running costs of £5,000.

In October 2006, the pace quickened. Harry

Barker, OS treasurer, announced the success of the appeal. Seventy-six generous members had pledged ongoing contributions totalling over £13,000 pa and 38 a one-off payment. An anonymous member had offered substantial potential help. One member mentioned the Rees Jeffreys Road Fund as being a possible source of funding the project.

Our solicitor prepared Terms for Renting the ground floor of The Wesleyan Chapel, Coalbrookdale, for the OS to consider. IGMT's agenda was to clear both upper and lower floors and decorate throughout. On this basis the OS might have been the tenant as from 1 June 2007. There was, however, mixed thinking and the author, in particular, was concerned about any short-term high-cost solution, when a deep storage default position would have been more viable. Notwithstanding, the L&ASC decided at its November 2006 meeting to recommend a 5(+5)-year lease on the renovated Chapel lower floor, subject to meeting rental and other conditions. This put in train interim plans which were not, in the event, needed.

At the November 2006 Council meeting, Harry Barker announced that, as a result of the appeal, a major benefactor had come forward who was willing to purchase a suitable building to the required specification, which would be rented to the OS at a modest rent. This was the best possible news for the Society.

It was still considered that five years would need to be bridged, despite the high cost this would have entailed. Indeed, there was still a risk that negotiations with IGMT might fail. The 1885 chapel building was also listed and had some structural defects. There was therefore concern over potential repairs and enforcement orders regarding its listed status. Notwithstanding the OS would enter into a five-year lease of the Chapel.

For the record, on three Wednesdays in late 2006, attendance by staff and researchers at Coalbrookdale averaged nearly 10 persons – it wasn't that remote for some! At Acton, things were not so busy – 'staff' numbers were low and regular opening dates were difficult to declare, but the site's capacity was being reached!

The shelves at Walsall contain a unique record of bus operation in the UK.

CHAPTER 3

Walsall

WALSALL – OUR NEW HOME?

In December, things moved even faster. On 7 December news came through that Alan Mills had located potential accommodation in Sandwell Street, Walsall, for rent or purchase, which matched our specification, both in size and location. Arrangements for a visit were made the following day. The author quickly re-visited his floor area calculations, arriving at 2,700sq ft based on allowing 2.5% natural growth, further major collections and the necessary computing and research areas. With retention of the 715sq ft in the Coalbrookdale Long Warehouse, a further 2,000sq ft would be ideal, taking a 17-20-year horizon.

On 11 December, the premises were inspected by Alan Mills; the author carried out preliminary measurements, plans were made and further enquiries pursued. On 12 January 2007, two senior officers of the Society and four Archive volunteers met with the benefactor to inspect the premises, retire to discuss findings and generally answer fit-for-purpose questions. As a result, our benefactor agreed to bid for the property.

By 12 February the author had prepared a critical path programme with planned 10-week closure of the library facility. The next day, an L&ASC meeting was held in Coalbrookdale to discuss whether we should still take up the ground floor offer at the Chapel. Despite the potential cash flow consequences, the meeting agreed to go ahead with the recommendation to rent the Chapel ground floor for a five-year term, there being concern that 'fitting out Walsall, assuming the bid was successful, might take years!'

The Library & Archive, Walsall premises, were officially opened by the OS 2007 President, Giles Fearnley, then chairman of Blazefield Holdings.

However, the 6 March Council, hearing that the benefactor was confident of bidding success, agreed that, in view of the above, the lease on the Chapel would not now be required. Instead, a four-month occupancy to the end of July had been negotiated.

Our 'deep-storage', the top floor of the Chapel, needed to be vacated by 29 March necessitating a large volunteer team to dust off and bring our material down to the vacated ground floor for sorting and re-allocation. Some of this material had not been looked at since its deposit there. On two days, 27 March and 10 April, working parties cleared the top floor of the

Outside 100 Sandwell Street, as acquired.
John Bennett

chapel, including the dismantling of 'insecure' shelving. This proved a dirty and demanding task – using a staircase human chain. At the end of the chain was Alan Mills, and the author considers that his sifting and sorting of the 'never-ending' stream of boxes and bundles was a most significant realisation of just what had been assembled over the years, which could now be placed in correct order at Walsall, or wherever it was destined. For the record, the team on those two days was: Alan Mills, Bob Gell, David Bean, Derek Broadhurst, Graham Harper, John Bennett, Maurice Collignon, Peter Hale, Peter Tulloch, Ron Thomas, Steve Ewald, Ted Gadsby, Ted Jones, Tony Drury and Wilf Dodds. There were now 112 days to the 31 July deadline of evacuation in order to sort out the archive tonnage on the downstairs floor! In a detail, the Westgate London cabinets would need to be taken to Acton.

On 11 May, the benefactor met three of the library staff for a last check prior to exchange of contracts, giving us much invaluable advice on maximising space, advantageous internal modifications, high shelving and erection of a mezzanine stage which, when carried out, added 500sq ft floor area – an extra 25%!

> At the end of the chain was Alan Mills, and the author considers that his sifting and sorting of the 'never-ending' stream of boxes and bundles was a most significant realisation of just what had been assembled over the years

KEYS, CRATES AND INCESSANT RAIN

On 14 May Alan Mills picked up the keys to 100 Sandwell Street and we made our first entry as tenant. With lots of hard work ahead, the prospects were exciting! On 18 May, the author measured up for a full floor plan, shelving and between-corridors being based on a 26in (660mm) module. The last week in May found the front and rear rooms of the former warehouse section (no.102) painted and newly carpeted, whilst the rear room false ceiling was removed. The mezzanine structure was ordered, shelving (10ft high) was designed and ordered, with all this being delivered and erected in the week beginning 25 June.

Early July found staff clearing up, removing the previous owner's redundant computing equipment and discussing the removal, for

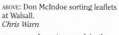

ABOVE: Don McIndoe sorting leaflets at Walsall.
Chris Warn

ABOVE LEFT: Inventory work in the Computer Room.

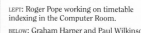

LEFT: Roger Pope working on timetable indexing in the Computer Room.

BELOW: Graham Harper and Paul Wilkinson in the sorting area at Walsall.
Ted Gadsby

The central area at Walsall, looking towards the Timetable room.

Journals, carefully boxed and indexed by Graham Harper.
Chris Warn

Carefully labelled boxes of timetables.
Chris Warn

The central area and mezzanine.
Chris Warn

which J Upton had been contracted. By 10 July, the air-conditioning plant was installed and electrician's work completed.

The removal started on 16 July. Over 300 crates were delivered to Coalbrookdale; N&Ps started the job; plus OS records and journals. On 17 July the first pantechnicon reached Walsall, whilst timetable boxes were loaded at Coalbrookdale. On 18 July many crates were unloaded at Walsall, including the loaned Monk Collection, whilst on 19 July, equipment was unloaded.

The author cannot resist but to relate the appalling state of the weather at this time. On 12 June, the Severn Valley Railway formation suffered a landslide, whilst on 25 June Kingston-upon-Hull enjoyed 117mm of rain and the Don Valley 12 days of torrential downpours. By the time of the removal, from 19-27 July, a second wave of excessive rain, incessant on Friday, 20 July, hit the Avon and Severn Valleys, causing widespread flooding at their Tewkesbury confluence. On this same day, unloading continued at Walsall, of Dethridge files, journals and more timetables. The following week Upton was clearing the chapel, a task completed by the 31 July deadline. The John Parke Memorial Library remained at Coalbrookdale for the time being.

After all this activity, it surprised us that Walsall was opened so quickly to members; last day at Coalbrookdale was 4 July, first at Walsall 22 August – only three weeks after the move! One reason for such a quick turn-round was in the planning. On 13/14 July all new Walsall shelves were labelled with a pre-determined number, along with positional identity. Then, every one of the 1,439 timetable boxes still at Coalbrookdale was given its pre-planned *destination* position. Schedules determined the intended location of other material. By this means, on unpacking the crates at Walsall, each box, having been marked with its new location, was lifted and placed into its exact correct position by the professional removers, saving us an enormous degree of physical effort.

A formal opening was planned. Firstly, 31 October was set aside for donors to inspect the facilities. 9 November 2007 was the Official Opening of the Library & Archive, Walsall premises, by the OS President, Giles Fearnley, chairman of Blazefield Holdings. Invited guests retired to the 'White Lion' for a celebratory buffet lunch.

> ❝
> … on unpacking the crates at Walsall, each box, having been marked with its new location, was lifted and placed into its exact correct position by the professional removers, saving us an enormous degree of physical effort

ARE WE THERE YET?

So, the OS archive has concluded a further phase of its history, with the Walsall premises having a remaining lease of around 20 years. In nearly five years since opening we have seen healthy researcher visits; the computer system and laptops find heavy use in indexing timetables, small operator listings (thanks to the late Chris Warn) and contents inventory. The challenge will now be to meet the change from paper to digital service information inflicted by local authority cuts, and to permit members remote access to these indices. Under Alan Mills, we regularly get help from John Batten, Geoff Budd, Ted Gadsby, Graham Harper, Don McIndoe, Roger Pope, Pat Russell, John Simpson, Desmond Southgate, Richard Ward and Paul Wilkinson.

The John Parke Memorial Library and the OSMART business remain in the hands of Derek Broadhurst at Coalbrookdale. Temporary occupation of the Darby Coach House there is necessitated by the current large wave of incoming material. His main sources of help come from Glyn Bowen, Mike Harper-Tarr, Ted Jones and Ron Thomas, as well as regular help from Walsall. Collections are still made from addresses in the United Kingdom, and attendance at rally stalls helps the funds.

Acton continues apace, under Martin Kingsnorth, with John Hart, John Marshall and Barry Wilkinson. Dave Bubier gives logistics help.

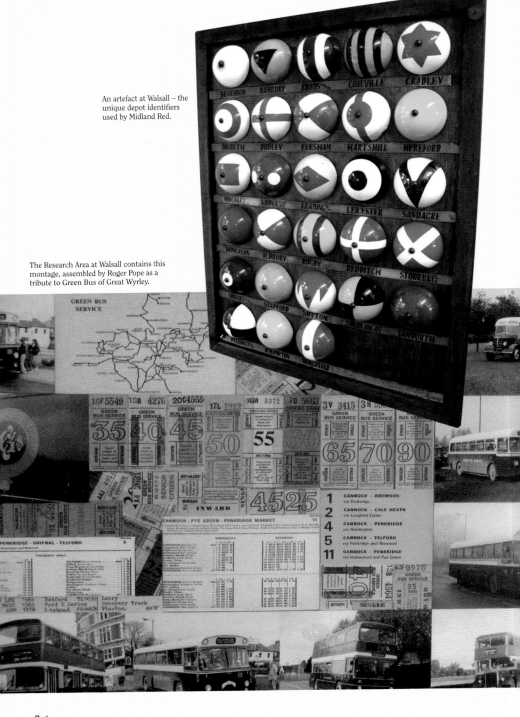

An artefact at Walsall – the unique depot identifiers used by Midland Red.

The Research Area at Walsall contains this montage, assembled by Roger Pope as a tribute to Green Bus of Great Wyrley.

Alan Oxley's post is now entitled photo archivist. John Bennett and Peter Tulloch ably assist providing back-up that includes the collection of material from various donors. Peter Badgery meticulously sorts and identifies photographs for cataloguing, Michael Eyre, assisted by Richard Morant, dedicatedly digitises, catalogues and indexes.

A print sale for members on the web-site has commenced. The section is expanding fast.

The ticket collection has been described in a talk in October 2007 by Rev Pat Lidgett, the hon curator, who continues to care for the collection after almost 20 years. Digitisation is now commencing to make this most valuable asset more accessible.

> ❝
> The challenge will now be to meet the change from paper to digital service information inflicted by local authority cuts, and to permit members remote access to these indices.

Running repairs to a United timetable.
Roger Pope

NOW REFLECT!

Writing this history may help to determine our future optimum management path. Continued *exponential* growth demands ever more *sustained* resources of time and money. For a guaranteed sustainable OS archive, we need to revisit our expected horizons, if its name is to mean anything in the *next* 70 years (even 20) – maybe more quality (retrieval, access, service) and only limited space-eating paper? At this 70th anniversary, perhaps in the end, this can be judged as the right time to have written this history, after a pause to consider the extraordinarily dedicated path it has so far taken.

EPILOGUE

As happens in recording history, events overtake the chronicler.

From a commissioned report by member Philip Kirk (MD of Oxford Bus Company) into the Archive's future, the Society will seek a professional archivist answerable to Council through an Archive Director (subject to the members ratifying a management restructure). A standardised website inventory is recommended; photographic sales are to be developed; accommodation expanded to permit centrally-held primary archives. OSMART is now fully incorporated into the Society.

Derek Giles' generous bequest will allow this. An Essex collection is part of his extensive and comprehensive legacy.

Four volunteers take a lunch break at Walsall.
Chris Warn

CHAPTER 4

The Archive Described

ARCHIVE HOLDINGS
A RESUMÉ OF WHAT IS HELD
Walsall

The provincial archive is held in Walsall and is the premier source for historical information on bus services in the United Kingdom and Ireland.

The Timetable Library is recognised by the British Library as being of national importance, covering timetables, leaflets, fareboooks, maps and guides produced by operators, authorities and publishers from late Victorian years to the present. Near-complete sets of the Traffic Commissioners' *Notices & Proceedings* covering all Traffic Areas from their start in 1931 to the present day are held.

The Archive holds company staff journals, accounts, annual reports, agreements and campaigns, and selected ledgers. Reports produced by government, local and shire councils as well as London Transport can be consulted, as can yearbooks.

Appropriate journals and associations proceedings from 1900 are kept. Relevant enthusiast magazines are retained, as are PSV Circle fleet publications.

OS official papers and Council Minutes are filed. News items include pre-WW2 Traffic News, all OS branch news reviews and bulletins, the *Omnibus Magazine* and numerous papers on subjects as diverse as 'London Bus organization in the C19' and 'Regional Transport Studies'.

Notable features are the collections donated by individuals. The Southgate Collection contains priceless source material on manufacturers and motor taxation. The Dethridge Collection consists of 200 files of operators' activities. The loaned Monk Collection, deals with Thomas Clarkson and the National Omnibus Company. Horse buses are recorded in the Sisley files.

The John F Parke Memorial Library contains over 7,000 books on the road passenger transport industry, together with legal and parliamentary documents and relevant research papers. This is the blossoming of the library referred to in the history text, and is very comprehensive, Although retained in Coalbrookdale, any book can be obtained via Walsall.

Martin Kingsnorth filing London material at Acton Depot.

Acton

The London Library is housed in the Acton Depot of the London Transport Museum. It contains a comprehensive collection of Central Bus and Country Bus and Green Line Coach (later LCBS and County Council) timetables, from the 1930s to date. There are Local and Country 'sector' books and Green Line Coach Guides. Some 'panel' timetables are retained, along with traffic circulars, service change leaflets, fare tables and maps. LT reports feature, including Chiswick engineers' vehicle records and 'Allocation Books' that provide scheduled frequencies and allocations of buses to each route. Staff publications, *Pennyfare, LT Magazine, LT News, LRT News* and *LT News (again)* are stocked. The Library also contains Metropolitan and South-Eastern Traffic Areas *Notices & Proceedings*, PSV Circle and LOTS publications.

The collection of Reg Westgate is extensive, covering London's transport history from the nineteenth century to the 1960s. Early steam carriages, horse bus operations and even street name-change files can be consulted. LGOC files are comprehensive, from vehicle type histories, allocations, changes and registration series (including Home Counties marks). Wartime loans and 1939 evacuation plans are interesting. Estate Department files describe garage management. Route numbering, operational data and changeovers files are held. Pre-1934 independents' vehicles and their premises information are included, along with valuable scrapbooks and year books covering events from 1898 to 1962. Chiswick Works and biographies are not neglected.

Indices and Source books

The Library maintains a broad index of items held at Walsall, Coalbrookdale and Acton which define their subject and location. Detailed sub-indices exist for operators' names (including the Master Operator Lists), time and fare tables, leaflets (very selective/numbered), journals, scrapbook contents, compact discs, etc. Many independent leaflets (pre-1940) and major operators (pre-1930) are held on microfiche.

Photographic Archive

Over the years photographs have been made available to members and most recently Alan Cross has supplied these from the collections of Charles Klapper, Ernest Masterman, John Cull, Alan Duke, John Parke and A W Mace. A photographic sales shop is now on the OS website, currently offering photographs taken by Maurice Norton, Neil McDonald, H J R Middleton and Pat Sparrow, all of whom thankfully catalogued and indexed their negatives, thereby making it easier for prospective purchasers. At the present time these images are only available to Society members.

Currently, it is estimated, there are 850,000 prints and slides plus 450,000 negatives of all sizes from glass to 35mm. CDs of images have also been donated along with DVDs and videos. These have come from the cameras of Ryan Carpenter, Wilf Dodds, Peter Henson (jointly with EMPTG), John Fielder, Ken Glazier (provincial), Dick Okill, Frank Riley, John Smith, Douglas Spray, Gerald Truran, Roger Wheal, Peter Yeomans and many more listed on the website. John Nickells, Tony Norris, and Reg Westgate collected many prints from various sources and with the West Yorkshire Information Service archive it covers the whole spectrum of the bus industry. Roy Marshall's colour slides are being digitised and indexed, whilst the collections of Geoffrey Morant and John Cockshott are being similarly treated.

A useful tool is the regular article in the OM under the 'From the Archives' title, from which much valuable identification of vehicles and locations has been gathered. The archive continues to grow and the aim is to make this the depository for a permanent national bus photo collection and perhaps you will consider donating your photographs which be held your in your name as a part of the overall scheme.

Ticket collection

The collection's roots go well back, as can be discerned from the history. Tickets have been catalogued and placed into albums. There are some 100,000 'Londons' and a similar number of Provincials – but less complete.

The London General Omnibus Company horse and early motorbus 1890-1908, London Road Car company 1882-1908, Metropolitan Electric Tramways and Croydon Tramways are largely comprehensive. An 1870 first-day issue is the oldest ticket held.

Much of the early provincial collection is, perhaps, southern-biased – tram tickets representing Bristol, Brighton, Bournemouth and Portsmouth. Bus tickets from East Kent, Maidstone & District and Southdown feature prominently. Some municipals feature well from the 1920s: (see 'Reinohl' and the main text for background to these early holdings).

London tickets are being remounted on acid-free paper in robust binders. The Provincials are based on pre-1974 counties, to be remounted, as for London. Consideration is being given to making catalogues available on the Internet, after scanning specific parts of the collection, but help may be needed.

The collection is held at the curator's house, in Alfreton, Derbyshire. Anyone wishing to study a part of the collection may do so in person, by appointment, or by reasonable request for sample photocopies of an operator's tickets.

The overseas ticket collection

Although the archive does not hold a comprehensive overseas collection, it retains some fascinating foreign bus and tram tickets from the early part of the twentieth century. As well as from varied parts of mainland Europe, there are notable examples of United Transport in Eastern and Southern Africa and other former parts of the British Empire. They help to portray the British influence at that time and allow us to understand the extent of the networks provided.

Initial assembly was by Reg Durrant, but for many years it has been in the care of Malcolm Chase. Currently lodged at Walsall.

'OSMART'

OSMART has been run since 1989 by Derek Broadhurst, providing a service for the purchase, sale and distribution of transport material of all kinds to enthusiasts at affordable prices. (See 'Who's who' for how it started).

OSMART is the designated principal agent for the handling of gifts and bequests to the OS. This involves travelling throughout the land by car or van to make collections and is a service that requires well-tuned antennae, speed, diplomacy and stamina. Material received often has to go through a lengthy process of carrying, sorting, selecting and pricing. Donors could reduce the severity of this task by keeping their intended bequests in an orderly manner, and advice can be given as to the library's systems.

Preference for purchase of material is given to the Library and a large proportion of the Archive since 1989 has come through Derek's hands in this way. In offering material for subsequent general sale, priority is given to OS members through the earlier dispatch to them of the OSMART catalogue, of which over 300 are sent out, prompting a demanding cycle of selection and drafting, parcelling and posting. Stan Letts and Maurice Collignon print and collate each catalogue.

An OSMART sales stand visits selected rallies and museums, with photographs now proving a robust turnover. Frequent financial donations are made to the Library & Archive from subscriptions and sales. The OS Treasurer receives periodic records of transactions between OSMART and the Society (Library).

WHY USE YOUR ARCHIVE?
Library WOW factors

Not all enquiries at the Library concern research, so what else has it been used for?

- A married couple had met on a coach travelling from Bristol to London, 50 years before; details were given of the exact journey they took.
- A government consultant studied timetables in order to report on changing bus service levels over different periods.
- People have come to study how their family entered the bus business, maybe in the 1920s.
- A young student studied the consequences of the 1930 Road Traffic Act.
- Exact departure time, route and operator from Blackburn was sought by researchers of a well-known Lakeland fell walker.
- and more…

VISITING ACTON

By agreement with the Acton Depot of the London Transport Museum, access for research is available on one day each week, currently Tuesdays, (OM or website for details). This is by prior arrangement, ideally a fortnight before your intended visit. Refreshments are not available on the site, so bring your own and you will be shown the area assigned for food and drink.

To reach the Acton Depot from Acton Town Station (District and Piccadilly lines in Zone 3) cross the road by the crossing, turn right, left into Museum Way; keep to the walkway and pass through large blue gates (if shut, press the 'Museum Depot' button), pass the ticket office and roller shutter loading bay; enter by the next door, where there is an entry phone to request access.

VISITING WALSALL

Access to the premises at 100 Sandwell Street, Walsall WS1 3EB is by prior arrangement only, usually on one regular day each week, currently Wednesdays – (OM or website for details). By bus from Birmingham (Carrs Lane area): National Express 51 (36 mins) or X51 (27 mins); alight at Six Ways, Walsall. Walk (westwards) up Lysways Street 250 yds, left at Sandwell Street; no.100 is 150 yds on right-hand side (set back).

By train from Birmingham; alight at Tame Bridge Parkway station. Walk up to the main road; left to traffic lights and cross the road. Catch the 404 (only) 'Walsall' (northwards) to Little London. This is the stop after the Sikh Temple on your right-hand side; on alighting, cross the road, walk back 50 yds to the (closed) 'Crown & Anchor' pub; turn left to climb 'Little London' (signpost missing) for 60 yds; bear slightly right for further 120 yds; at the 'White Lion' turn left and climb Sandwell Street for 220 yds; no.100 is on the left-hand side (set back).

For directions by car, use the postcode or ask us for a map. National Cycle Route 5 passes our entrance; the only person to cycle here is Jack Haddock (born September 1927), a local transport historian from Birchills and friend of the OS.

Queries can be made through www.omnibussoc.org or e-mail oslibrary@btconnect.com. Telephone number is 01922 629358 for emergency or brief use. Please do not expect lengthy queries to be solved by telephone. Telephone and e-mail are only responded to on Library days.

Bring your own lunch, or expect to walk 500 yds in search of food. There are strict rules with regard to eating/drinking near to research material. Hot drinks are available, and a contribution towards costs is welcome.

Remember your membership number for signing in, and record the subject of your research. Please read the rules for researchers, and understand copyright restrictions if publishing is in mind; laptop use is permitted, but ask if you wish to use a camera or scanner; a copying machine is available, a price list for copying is displayed.

STORAGE AND CONSERVATION

Standard Boxes: A standard set of boxes was designed and the first brought into use in May 1999. There are three heights – 6in, 4in and 2in. In plan they fit A4 paper lying flat, the 6in take A5 on edge and the 4in the popular Slimline (A4/3) on edge. Other material was placed into 2in boxes until the space at Coalbrookdale became so tight as to justify the replacement of any box less than half full by conservation wallets. Wallets also allow for filing foolscap and like-sizes. The same boxes are used at Acton, Coalbrookdale and Walsall, and lids are common to all sizes, allowing flexibility in their use. Each box is assembled from flat packs; to date, over 3,000 have been personally assembled, with 2,000 in use at Walsall and the rest at Acton and Coalbrookdale.

Conservation: In 2002, the conservation of fragile leaflets into archive-approved sleeving was commenced. Paper quality has varied over the years and degradation is not only attributable to age or storage environment. Many prewar papers are in good condition, but those of the 1920s, World War 2 examples and Suez Crisis periods are poor. Lack of volunteers for this work has meant only slow progress.

Repairs: Many of the tiny format timetables of the late 1920s and early 1930s, which hid in people's pockets and had enthusiastic regular use, are in need of 'surgery'. This is another time-consuming slow job, but needs to be done. Fortunately, the contents are microfiched, which reduces their direct handling.

HELP, IT'S FUN

What skills do you have that can help develop the service provided?

Inventorising is a two-stage process. We still need painstaking detailed listing of much library archive material. Or, perhaps you prefer to use your IT skills to assemble these for website access?

PDF timetables: We require members in all geographical areas to download timetables and other service literature. A standard system is set up for capturing such data.

Scanning of tickets: As we embark on this, have you the interest to be part of a small team?

Photographs: Do you have a regional or operator-specific interest? Perhaps you would like to join Alan Oxley's team in his quest to provide the best UK photo archive.

Conservation and preservation: Do you have the patience to repair torn or split paper material, or gently file away fragile leaflets within approved sleeves?

OSMART provides one of the main arteries of OS activity. Perhaps you can assist as a regional agent in a chain to collect, hold or forward material or assist in listing leaflets for eventual sale. Like to assist us at show stalls? Let Derek Broadhurst know.

Contact details: If you can identify any way you could assist, or think you could manage things better yourself, contact one of the Library, Photographic or Ticket Archivists, or write to the Librarian & Archivist (with your membership number if 'new' to us) at the Sandwell Street address, or e-mail oslibrary@btconnect.com. We look forward to hearing your ideas.

CHAPTER 5

The People

OMNIBUS SOCIETY PRESIDENTS

1947	Sidney E Grackle CBE *Director, East Kent Road Car Co Ltd.*	1978	F Philip Groves *General Manager, Nottingham City Transport*
1948	Charles E Lee *Assistant to Managing Director, Tothill Press*	1979	Robert Brook *Deputy Chairman & Chief Executive, National Bus Company*
1949	Alfred Baynton OBE *General Manager, East Kent Road Car Co Ltd*	1980	Ian Cunningham *General Manager, Bournemouth Transport*
1950	Charles F Klapper *Associate Editor, Modern Transport*	1981	John F Parke *Managing Editor, Buses*
1951	Col Sir Joseph Nall BART., DSO, OBE *Chairman, Llandudno & Colwyn Bay Electric Railway*	1982	James Isaac *Director General, West Midlands PTE*
1952	Major F J Chapple DSO, OBE *General Manager, Bristol Tramways & Carriage Co Ltd*	1983	Ian S Irwin CBE *Managing Director, Scottish Transport Group*
		1984	Geoffrey Steele *Operations Director, Wallace Arnold Tours*
1953	Donald M Sinclair CBE *General Manager, Birmingham & Midland Motor Omnibus Co Ltd*	1985	David Hargreaves *Chairman & Managing Director, Hestair plc*
1954	John M Birch *Deputy Chairman and General Manager, Birch Bros Ltd*	1986	Werner W Heubeck OBE *Managing Director, Ulsterbus Ltd*
1955	W J Crosland-Taylor MC *Director & General Manager, Crosville Motor Services*	1987	G Eric Hutchinson *Managing Director, Busways Travel Service*
		1988	Trevor Smallwood *Group Managing Director, Badgerline Holdings Ltd.*
1956	John B Burnell CBE *Operating Manager, Central Road Services, London Transport Executive*	1989	Derek L Fytche *Chairman, Natpro Ltd/London Country Bus (NW) Ltd.*
1957	Charles W Baroth *General Manager, Salford City Transport*	1990	Barry Moore *Managing Director & Vice Chairman, Ipswich Buses Ltd*
1958	Raymond W Birch CBE *Chairman, Yorkshire Traction Co Ltd*	1991	Robert Smith *Transport Executive, Isle of Man Transport*
1959	Norman Morton *General Manager, Sunderland Corporation Transport*	1992	Brian King *Chairman & Managing Director, Wellglade Ltd, Barton Buses Ltd, Trent Motor Traction Ltd*
1960	Sir William Black *Managing Director, ACV Group Ltd.*	1993	Mervyn Pugh *Traffic Commissioner, West Midlands and South Wales Traffic Areas*
1961	W M Little *Transport Manager, Edinburgh Corporation Transport*		
1962	T W H Gailey CBE *Chairman, United Automobile Services Ltd*	1994	Andre Testa *General Manager, Noord-Zuid Hollandse Vervoer Maatschappij NV*
1963	E L Taylor OBE *Chairman, Western Welsh Omnibus Co Ltd*		
1964	Norman H Dean OBE *General Manager, Yorkshire Traction Co Ltd*	1995	Sandy Glennie *Chief Executive, Volvo Truck & Bus (UK)*
1965	R M Robbins *Chief Commercial and Public Relations Officer, London Transport Executive*	1996	Peter Shipp *Joint Managing Director, EYMS Group Ltd*
		1997	Charles Marshall *(former) Managing Director, OK Travel Ltd*
1966	W M Dravers TD *Chairman, Devon General Omnibus & Touring Co Ltd.*	1998	Brian Fisher *Managing Director, Plymouth Citybus Ltd*
		1999	Stephen C Morris *Editor, Buses*
1967	Chaceley T Humpidge *General Manager, Sheffield Transport Department*	2000	Ron Whittle OBE *Chairman, Whittle Holidays & Coaches*
1968	E Arthur Lainson *Chairman & Managing Director, Premier Travel Ltd*	2001	Moir Lockhead OBE *Chief Executive, FirstGroup*
1969	Bernard Griffiths *Chairman, South Wales Transport Co Ltd*	2002	Peter Bell *Managing Director, Preston Bus*
1970	Michael J McCoy *Operating Manager, Central Buses, London Transport*	2003	Ted Hesketh CBE *Managing Director, Group Operations, Translink*
		2004	Peter Hendy *Managing Director, Surface Transport, Transport for London*
1971	Albert Burrows *Director General, Merseyside PTE*		
1972	J T E Robinson *Chairman, South Wales and West Region, National Bus Company*	2005	John Owen *Managing Director, Thamesdown Transport Ltd*
		2006	Chris Moyes OBE *Chief Executive, Go-Ahead Group*
1973	Leslie H Smith TD, DL — *General Manager, Leicester City Transport*	2007	Giles Fearnley *Chief Executive, Blazefield Group/North Bus Operations, Transdev plc*
1974	Ronald Cox *Director General, Greater Glasgow PTE*		
1975	David S Deacon *Group Executive (Special Duties), National Bus Company*	2008	Gavin Booth *Chairman, Bus Users UK*
		2009	Philip W Kirk *Managing Director, The Oxford Bus Company*
1976	Robert Bailey *Director & General Manager, Lancashire United Transport Ltd*	2010	Mark Howarth *Managing Director, Western Greyhound Ltd*
		2011	Francois–Xavier Perin *Transport Consultant (formerly Managing Director, Transdev Group)*
1977	J Graeme Bruce *Operating Manager (Railways), London Transport Executive*	2012	Roger French OBE *Managing Director, Brighton & Hove Bus & Coach*

OFFICE HOLDERS

Omnibus Society Chairmen
1929-1947	Charles E Lee
1947-1949	Charles Klapper
1949-1952	Eric Osborne
1952-1963	Graeme Bruce
1963-1966	Bill Lambden
1966-1973	John Parke
1973-1981	Tom McLachlan
1981-1984	John Fielder
1984-2011	Barry Le Jeune
2011-	Stephen Morris

Hon Secretaries
1929-1946	Charles Klapper
1947-1951	John Parke
1952-1957	William Street
1958-1966	Douglas Spray
1966-1969	Bernard Wintle
1971-1978	Marcus Gaywood
1979-1986	Reg Westgate
1987	Geoff Morant
1988-2000	Brian Chappell
2000-	Tony Francis

Central Timetable Curator
1942-1949	John Parke
1950-1963	Reg and Mrs D E Durrant
1964-1993	Brian Walter

Memorial Librarian
1976-1980	Tom Smith
1980-1981	Chris Goodwyn
1982-1993	Brian Walter

Photographic registrar
(not continuous)
1942	Edgar Sharpe
1950-1958	Joe Higham
1958	J P Ramsey
1959-1970	David Simpson
1973	Arnold Mason
1982	Malcolm Papes

Hon Treasurers
1929-1934	Noel Jackson
1934-1942	E Moffatt
1943-1948	Edgar Sharpe
1949-1970	Jimmy Blair
1971-1984	Terry Dendy
1985-1987	Geoffrey Morant
1989	Harry Barker

Photographic curator and printer
1993-	Alan Cross

Photographic Archivist
2005	Peter Tulloch
2006-	Alan Oxley

Librarian
1945-1954	John Parke
1954-1956	John Hibbs
1956-1959	Peter Gerhold
1960	Alfred Hendrie
1961-1971	Geoffrey Brockington
1971-1993	John Smith

Ladbroke Grove manager
1958	M H Ford
1959	John Gillham

London collection curator
1993-2009	John Hart
2009	Martin Kingsnorth

Ticket curator
1946-1993	Reg Durrant
1993-	Rev Pat Lidgett

Overseas ticket minder
1989-2010	Malcolm Chase

Librarian and Archivist
1993-	Alan Mills

Editors of the Omnibus Magazine
Without whom much historical information would have gone unrecorded.

Issue no.	Cover dates	Editor
1-48	1/30-12/33	Charles Klapper (collator)
49-60	1/34-12/34	Charles Klapper (glossy publication)
'Q1'–'Q4'	3/35-12/35	Charles Klapper (glossy publication)
61-66	1/35-6/35	Charles Klapper (collator)
67-75	3/39-4/40	Charles Klapper (collator)
(Info Sheets)	5/38-3/43	(Klapper/La Croix/Gillham/Parke)
76-78	11/46-3/47	Klapper/Parke
(79)	9/51	(news-sheet only)
80-103	3/52-12/56	Eric Osborne
104-111	1-9/57	Brian Knowlman
112-128	10/57-2/59	John W Taylor
129-223	3/59-3/67	Ken Swallow
224-240	4/67-9/68	Mervyn Banks
241-275	10/68-12/71	Gavin Booth (I)
276-336	1/72-1/82	Peter R White
337-348	3/82-Spring/84	John F Parke
349/350	As Co-ordinator	Geoff Morant
351-367	Winter/84-Winter/88	Alan Bates
368-371	Transition role	Tony Francis
372-395	Spring/90-5/94	Gavin Booth (II)
396-435	6/94-12/00	Joint editors
		Dave Bubier
		(+ as associate editor to 12/06)
		Oliver Howarth
		(as associate editor to 10/08)
436-471	2/01-12/06	Brendan Chandler
		(continues as Assistant compiler)
472/473	Transition role	Stephen Morris
474-date	6/07-date	Cyril McIntyre

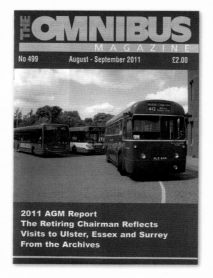

WHO'S WHO?

Brief details of selected members mentioned in the history and the lists of society officers. (Locations shown are a residential snapshot)

Listing by original membership entry, those who had joined by the 'unfrozen' 1942 watershed

Charles Edward Lee (Central London) b.1901, CIMarineEng, ecclesiology brain; OS co-founder; 1931 Council; Chairman until 1947; President 1948; OM322; 'Characters of the Bus Industry', 2004; d.1983 obit OM347.

Charles F Klapper (Bromley) b.1905, co-founder; 1931 Council; Hon Sec until 1947 and Publications Officer; Chairman 1947-49; President 1950; 'Characters of the Bus Industry'; OM284, 322; d.1980 obit OM325

William Noel Jackson (Cranleigh) b.1904, keen photographer; co-founder; 1931 Council; Treasurer 1931-34; OM322, 370; d.1989 obit OM371.

Edward Melville Stanley Upton (London SE) b.1907; IR valuer; avid ticket and timetable collector; 1931 Council; d. accidentally 1962 obit OM175.

Ronald Richard John Plummer b.1906, co-founder; presumed to have used 'W T Turner' as a pseudonym; LMSR-BR-THC career; d.1991 no obit.

John H Fielder (Wimbledon) b.c.1914, co-founder (as junior); LGOC Chiswick apprentice 1930; OM 322; ed. *Passenger Transport, Transport World*, chairman 1981-84; OM370; d.1996 obit OM411.

F J Grimoldby (Grimsby), b.1880, Council member; still known to be alive in 1967.

Paul Gomes (Dunstable/Harpenden); ed. 'ABC Coach Guide' at Index Publishers (see footnote); postal circuit administrator; later Secretary of the Isle of Wight Steam Railway; OM370; d.1992 obit OM384.

Joe F Higham (Middlesex), doyen of London matters esp. 1924-34 independents; photographer; d.1974 obit OM293.

Eric Nathan Osborne (Bushey Heath); Index Publishers; Jersey bus expert; trained as pilot in the Civil Air Guard; Chairman 1949-51, OM ed. 1952-56; d.1979 obit OM319.

Leslie Melville R Nicholson (Bromley), b.1905; 1931 Council; papers expert; paddle steamer fan; route recording scheme organiser; d.1980 obit OM326.

H (Bert) G Chambers (Smethwick, SE London), lorries interest; Council.

Marcus Gaywood (inc.Redhill, Fleetwood, Llandaff) b.1904; vehicle recorder; first Hon Sec South Wales & West Branch, d. 1994 obit OM399.

Ernest GP Masterman, early vehicle photographer, PoW 1941-45; d.1987 obit OM362

H G Baker JP, 1932 member, ticket enthusiast.

Alec G Jenson MBE, architect, lifetime researcher, President Birmingham Transport Historical Group; d.1982 announced OM339.

E Moffatt (SW London); Treasurer from 1934 until killed in a 1942 air-raid, frustrating several years-worth of accounts.

George H Bullock (Sheffield), Active from 1932, Yorkshire route recorder; d.1964 obit OM187.

Iolo Watkin (Dunstable); Index Publishers (see footnote); effected major 1937 input to the future ticket collection; he recollected earliest members.

John Garrard (Jack) Baker (Cheam, Warrington (ICI), Frodsham); joined 1933 with Cecil Smithies (qv); serial bus rider; d.1981 obit 334.

Cyril A Tibbett, MD Index Publishers (see footnote)

Douglas H D Spray (Streatham), Hon.Sec. 1958-66; OM370, d.1997 obit OM418.

Peter Laurence Hardy (New Brighton, Birmingham, Lyme Regis) b.1915; GWR fan; Branches pioneer 1936 & 1946; Pioneer Veh Rec (pre-WW2); BMMO officer and prolific researcher; Birmingham THG; d.1986 obit OM360.

John Thornton King (Purley/Beckenham), route recorder; d.1983, obit 344.

Henry John Corner, died on active service in the Middle East, 1942. His timetable collection, along with Parke's, founded the OS collection.

John C Gillham (Gunnersbury Park, Ealing); wartime news-sheets; doyen mapper, itinerary expert, 24hr clock objector; d.2009 obit OM486.

James Kinloch Dalgleish Blair (Stanmore), Hon Treasurer, prolific vehicle and route recorder esp.Scottish; d.1979 obit OM318.

Alan Duke CBE, (Finchley), b.1920; PoW (Italian hands) in WWII; vehicle recorder, Eastern/London; motor tax record holder; d.1993 obit OM392.

A V P (Jimmy) LaCroix (Chichester, Brighton); 'master' vehicle recorder, press cuttings and observations collator; d.1961 obit OM157.

Bernard Phillips Early veh recr lost during the fall of Singapore; OM 8/42.

Edgar Herbert Vercoe Sharpe (Harrow, Manchester); AEC and United Automobile Services enthusiast, first Photographic Registrar and Hon Treas 1943-48; d.1998 obit OM424.

Footnote: Paul Gomes, ed 'ABC Coach Guide' is known to have worked, at Index Publishers, alongside Cyril and Gordon Tibbett, Eric Osborne, John Webster, Iolo Watkin and Edgar Sharpe (and later Alan Bates). However, the reconstructed pre-1942 membership list shows 'J A Tibbett', otherwise unknown, but a postwar list does shows him as 'C A Tibbett', believed to be Cyril Tibbett, Managing Director, Index Publishers.

Post-1942 selected members mentioned in the text (These are still in membership entry order)

George Cookson b.1908; (Preston); expert on Pilgrim Motors., Ribble MS and other Lancashire operators; timetable collector; d.1997 obit OM412.

J Graeme Bruce OBE (Harrow); London Transport Chief Operating Manager (Railways); Route rec. Scotland; Chairman 1952-63; OM173,370; Pres.1977; d.2001 obit OM439.

A Stanley Denton (Bradford, Hull, Coventry), b.1918; Theses inc. early Bradford operators; d.1991 obit OM379.

Peter K Gerhold (SW London, Axminster); Librarian 1956-59.

W (Bill) T Lambden (Farnborough); Chairman 1963-66; General Manager Isle of Man National Transport, d.1978 (OM315).

William J C Street (Watford); Hon. Sec. 1952-57.

David J Simpson (Sanderstead, Virginia USA); Photographic Registrar 1959-70; master indexer of journals, enthusiast magazines & OM (pub.P1).

Bernard H Wintle Sqn.Ldr.(Ramsgate); Hon. Sec.1966-69; d.1984 obit OM352.

George Juxon Robbins b.1909; (London); London Bus History Study Group; d.2002 obit OM444.

Alan Bates, another at Index Publishers; Ed OM 1984-88; d.1994.

Ken Glazier (London SE). London expert and writer; obit OM473.

John S Cockshott (Bradford, Windsor), photographer, vehicle recorder, PSV Circle Chairman, staunch active Council member; d.1990, obit. OM374.

J P Ramsey (Sydenham); short-term Photographic Registrar (1958/59).

Geoffrey G Brockington (Isleworth) b.1935; Librarian from 1961-71.

Alfred R Hendrie (Central London) b.1938; short-period (1961) Librarian.

Rev Eric Ogden (North West), Assistant Photographic Registrar 1966-70, PSV Circle Librarian; d.2011 obit *The Guardian* 6/2/11, Buses 671.

Frank Dean Simpson (London/Brentwood/Exmouth), b.1910; Independent operator guru; researcher/publisher; d.2002 obit OM449.

Tom H Smith (London, Louth); Memorial Librarian 1976-80.

Geoffrey William Morant, b.1928; Hon. Sec & Treasurer, 1987 era; Buses Worldwide interests; d.2006 obit OM472.

Gerald Truran, photographer; collection held at Long Eaton; d.2005 obit OM462.

EIGHT MAJOR DONORS

J Cecil H Smithies (Cheshire) joined in 1933 along with his school friend from Christ's Hospital, Jack Baker. They both worked at ICI and were 'serial' bus riders. A pioneer member of the NW branch. Cecil Smithies compiled a comprehensive list of bus operators in England and Wales (but excluding London), up to around 1963, from company registers, directories, year books and timetables. Subsequently, in OS hands, the list was divided into counties; the PSV Circle was also involved (see text for details). These lists are known as 'Master Operators' Lists'. Mention should be made of another 'Smithies List', in the possession of the Roads & Roads Transport History Association, which is being used as a separate companies database (PHRG bulletin 108 refers).

Alfred William Monk (Essex), b.1912, d.1995 obit OM406. A 1935 member, resigning when called up for war service, he was known for his intense interest in the National Omnibus & Transport Co Ltd. and its successors, accumulating much material on Thomas Clarkson, its founder, and his steam buses. Meticulous historical records enabled him to be a major contributor to the three-volume history 'The Years Between, 1909-1969'. He had a fondness for City coaches and Southend operations. By kind permission of his son Roger, his collection is on long-term loan to the archive, being held at Walsall.

W Leonard Cox (Gloucestershire, Cambridge, Kent, South Croydon), b.1917; d.1942 obit OM 8/42. Short-lived Leonard Cox had such potential. The methodical schoolboy persuaded major operators to provide him with their fleet lists. With John Parke, he instigated a network of individuals who produced nationwide fleet records written into little black books. He joined the OS in 1936. Graduating at Cambridge University he applied a mathematical approach to timetables and rosters as a scheduler with Maidstone & District Motor Services. From 1938 he convinced Council to open up communications with the membership, setting a base for the introduction of an accessible archive, being elected to Council in 1939. In a brief period, during RAF training, he wrote comprehensive reports on transport operations wherever he encamped, including the Isle of Man in late 1940, the Shetland Islands in 1941 and in Northern Ireland was able to amass data from many Irish operators, including rare independents. Posthumously, all this fed into the black books. Tragically, it ended when, in 1942, Flight Lieutenant Cox died in an aircraft that disappeared without trace. His records were entrusted to John Parke, permitting Jimmy LaCroix to develop them after the war, providing data for early Fleet Histories.

Reginald G Westgate (London, St Albans, Nottingham): Recollections OM 370; d.2005 obit OM466. Reg, who joined the OS in 1938, was an assiduous researcher, producing the 'monumental' first two volumes of 'London Buses', charting the history of the London independent operators of the 1920s and early 1930s, and he was a contributor to 'Motor Omnibus Routes in London'. For years he was a member of Council, being Secretary for a long period, committee member of the Herts & Beds Group, Secretary of the London Historical Research Group (LHRG) and later a Group Convenor. He was a prime mover in the establishment of the Provincial Historical Research Group (PHRG). In the context of the archive he established the proper constitution of the Library & Archive sub-committee from 1993, acting as its Secretary for the remaining 12 years of his life. His very extensive London Transport records are held at Acton (see 'Archive holdings)', and those of provincial operators and general transport matters are at Walsall. Reg was always willing to share his information with others and was one of life's gentlemen.

John Edward Dunabin (Warrington) b.1916; d.2002 obit OM448. John's membership went back to 1946. He was the original organiser of the OM timetable news. His unique researches and his pen produced numerous interesting presentations on independent operators as far apart as Herefordshire, Stockton Heath, Leyland and Teesdale. He served on the North Western & Yorkshire Branch committee. In 1985, he founded the Provincial Historical Research Group providing the forum for exchange of ideas on research and researching. Other interests covered the Kilvert Society, the theatre and church architecture – perhaps these broad passions giving some idea of his value as 'the complete man'. John was researching the Tocia Motor Omnibus history at the time of his death, now published posthumously. His gentle nature and deep knowledge is still remembered with affection by many. Walsall holds much of his archive.

Derrick Selby Giles (Westcliff-on-Sea), b.1930; d.2010 obit OM494, *Buses* and trade press. Derek was an active local member for years, having joined in 1949, serving on Council from the 1950s and unselfishly representing the interests of others. In later years he briefly chaired the PHRG and administered its publications. Often focusing his calculating mind on longer-term goals, he proved invaluable at steering through the relevance of Parliamentary Acts and statutory obligations in which others were confused. Profoundly helpful to the Library, he scoured Science Museum records on our behalf and often turned up at memorabilia auctions. For decades he collected material from the industry, with his inside knowledge, and bequeathed a legacy (subject to probate) of his South Essex Collection and much more to the OS. Remembered as the kindly bachelor who lived all his life in his former parents' Essex bungalow, close by Westcliff Station, he rose monthly at 3.00am using unadvertised rail and tube connections that only he could devise and turning up at Coalbrookdale or Walsall before 'us Midlanders'! His contribution can only be evaluated with the passage of time.

Tom H J Dethridge (Epsom) Compiler of 'The Dethridge files' (OM274). The Library contains some 200 scrapbooks, an oft-used source of research, which he assembled. Researching at Ladbroke Grove around 1964, he was shown several dusty boxes containing press cuttings of transport interest. Chiefly, but not solely, amongst these was the work of Jimmy LaCroix ranging from 1928 to 1950. He took on the role of sorting material from all the boxes methodically, by re-assembling the contents into regions for larger operators and Counties for the smaller operators down to the one-person businesses. The results were pasted onto paper sheets and retained in foolscap ring-files. He soon decided to expand it bringing the system up to date (early 1970s) and, by adding to the files over the forthcoming years, a geographical balance was achieved. His files are retained intact as he presented them. He remains a valued current member.

Desmond Southgate We owe Desmond our gratitude for the provision of motor tax records, and history of motorbus chassis makers from the earliest years. His motor tax records, covering much of the West Midlands and further, abstracted in the 1950s-1970s, helped form the 'database' from which the assembled order of chassis listings could be accomplished. Manufacturers themselves, or their successors or descendants, were interviewed to extract much history that would otherwise have never been recorded, Maudslay being an example, including his interest in their engines. He recorded tales he heard of three-day journeys taking Halley chassis from Yoker to London, and the reverse movement of Great War chassis being driven back to North Britain for use as trucks/charabancs. He still liaises with museums (Coventry, Gaydon) on matters of allied history. Desmond is a regular volunteer at Walsall.

EIGHT NOTABLE CURATORS

Reginald J Durrant (Orpington) b.1911; d.1994 obit OM398 – Rev Pat Lidgett being involved in scattering his ashes off Beachy Head. Stories abound – he collected tickets from around the UK; in the bank where he worked he established collection boxes (in more than one branch) for tickets in aid of the Children's Hospital, but diligently removed what he needed from the box before it was passed on! His parents were not keen on his collecting tickets, so these were kept in a shed. During WWII the shed was destroyed in an air raid, and only a few tickets were salvaged. It was also during the war that he suffered an accident whilst driving for the army, which was the cause of one of his legs being shorter than the other. At the end of the war, he was posted to Germany, where he was placed in charge of the NAAFI, whereon he ordered coloured tickets from 'Bell Punch' as meal tokens! One of the earliest OS members, he had joined in 1932. He was a Council member and its Membership Secretary for years, distributing journals and news sheets to members. He was at one time President of the Transport Ticket Society. Reg nurtured the OS Ticket Collection (see OM163), which grew out of his own prewar private collection, from 1946 to 1993, and housed the timetable collection for many years, using racks in his spacious loft at Petts Wood. Mrs D E Durrant administered the postal side of this during the 1950s. He studied and recorded London bus routes, being Route Recorder. The multiple references to his name in the text, notably as curator of our timetables and tickets for so many years, prove a testimony to his work on our behalf, latterly being elected a Vice President. (Thanks to Rev.Pat Lidgett for part of the above).

John F Parke (Sevenoaks) b. 1916 d.1994 obits OM396 Buses 471.

John was a 1933 member and it was he who laid down the idea and early foundations of the archive in 1942, coincident with his election to Council and appointment as Assistant Publications Secretary. He was knowledgeable on transport in general, including aviation, from way back in 1934, when, as a young man, he took on the long-term role of transport correspondent to the *Kent & Sussex Courier*, which must have given him a good feel about the importance of timetables. We remember him as editor of *Modern Transport* and, after its Ian Allan takeover, of *Buses (Illustrated)* from 1963-1981. He was Secretary of the OS from 1947-1951, its Chairman from 1966-1973 and its 1981 President and even had a late spell as OM editor from 1982-1984. In the 1970s he was Secretary to the Transport Trust. In later years his diabetes and loss of both legs never dampened his enthusiasm for the OS. His death at the same time as the opening of the Coalbrookdale site was a shock to us. Described as an English Gentleman, the OS is gratified to have dedicated the Memorial Library in his name.

Brian L Walter (Hounslow) d.2002 obit OM444. After joining the OS in 1952, Brian superintended the timetable collection (initially under Reg Durrant) from 1964 until 1993, taking on the Memorial Library as well, from January 1982. He was the contact for postal loans of these items, an arduous feature being the reluctance of borrowers to return items. At Ladbroke Grove, Brian assisted all researchers, replying promptly to requests, apologising for delays, and was always courteous and conforming. His records of the loans were meticulous. In his obituary, John Dunabin wrote: '*the OS owes its continued existence and success to the labours of many people, some of them remaining well in the background. Brian was an honourable member of that number.*'

John George Springall Smith (Brookmans Park) b.1928; d.2002 obit OM446. John became a member in 1965. Career-wise he was involved in London underground signalling and other electrical engineering commitments. A prolific bus photographer of the London scene, provincial operators and signal boxes, his collection is now held at Long Eaton. In 1971 he was appointed Hon Librarian and embarked on a written resumé of the state and development of that part of the archive. He remained in charge and spent many hours organising the collections at Ladbroke Grove and later at the various sites to which it was scattered, before the move to Coalbrookdale. This, 1993, was when he retired from the post. The Library would not be in its present well organised state, but for his diligence and dedication.

Wilf Harry Dodds (Wolverhampton, Lancashire, Nuneaton) b.1940; d.2010 obit OM491. In the 1950s, Wilf travelled the country with Alan Mills abstracting Local Authority motor tax records, often stored in filthy basements, thus providing a database of knowledge for vehicles from the 1920s to 1950s. His loves were Leyland Motors, Ribble and Don Everall. Joining OS in 1971, he latterly managed our journals, company records and staff bulletins, searching to fill omissions and recording it all for easy retrieval. He served as Secretary of Midland Branch 1985-2003 and PHRG Treasurer 2003-10. He gave enormous help to Derek Broadhurst, sold photographs at rally stalls, and travelled throughout the land to pick up collections of material for the archive and OSMART. Latterly, Wilf formed a lone link between Coalbrookdale and Walsall. His sudden death in 2010 caused a quick re-appraisal of filling the large gap he had left.

John C Hart first assisted at Ladbroke Grove in 1983 and was then heavily involved in the transfer of material to various sites on its closure, subsequent removals to Coalbrookdale, and recovery of the London Collection to its late-1999 venue at the Acton Museum Depot. He played a significant role in planning and effecting these movements. The complication of accounting for, recovering and placing material, once scattered in private houses, LT garages and the Coalbrookdale Wesleyan Chapel, does him great credit. John's prolific cataloguing of all UK and Ireland's timetables and leaflets during the 1990s forms the basis of the catalogues held at both Acton and Walsall. He held the title of London Librarian until June 2009, remains a key volunteer and periodically manages the inter-transfer of items between London and the West Midlands.

66

Wilf's loves were Leyland Motors, Ribble…

Derek A Broadhurst has been a member since 1964. His idea for 'OSMART' started on one regular visit to his local (Staffordshire) second-hand bookshop and being directed to a pile of books and magazines, just purchased from a recently widowed lady. Searching through the magazines, he discovered a quantity of *Omnibus Magazines*, from which dropped an OS membership card. Speaking to the widow later, he was shocked to learn that she had been paid a derisory amount for her husband's collection. This set him thinking: why couldn't the OS have a system whereby such collections could be distributed around the membership and, if necessary, relatives paid a fair sum for them? Trials began with Midland Branch, (Stan Letts' suggesting a title 'OSMART') – the rest is recorded in this history. Although his own brainchild, Derek acknowledges the help given in the past by his cousin, David Broadhurst, and more recently by Wilf Dodds, both have now sadly passed away.

Derek's stories reflect on the situations he encounters on our behalf. Arriving at a widow's house he found a few stacks of hard-backed transport books neatly laid out. Knowing that the deceased husband had been an avid timetable collector, he asked 'Is there anything else?' On being directed outside, a large number of black sacks were lined up against the dustbin. These contained hundreds of timetables, some dating back to the 1920s. Had he arrived the following day, they would have disappeared to the local tip!

Visiting a house, he found it full of transport effects, with the occupants living in a corner of one room. It was necessary to shuffle sideways up the stairs, with magazines and books piled on each step, and every spare living space used for storage! Derek's work includes curatorship of the Memorial Library which, at the time of writing, remains at Coalbrookdale. Here, also, are housed provincial timetable booklets second copies (up to 1974). His unrelenting hard work for the Society is encapsulated in the narrative, from 1988 to the present day. A profile was given in OM481/482.

Alan Mills, the driving force behind the OS Library & Archive. *Chris Warn*

Alan W Mills Perhaps only when a sequel to this history is written will the contribution of Alan in developing our archive be appreciated and put into perspective. The author hopes it suffice to say that since assuming the role of Deputy Chairman of the OS around 1980, he has shown a single-minded dedication to the assembly, development and integration of the archive. We all take advantage of his extensive knowledge and sharp recall of many avenues of passenger transport history. Perhaps it is the once-headmaster in him that motivates volunteers into a sense of their own autonomy, giving us inspiration and making our work an enjoyable pastime.

And: Let us hope that a sequel to this history will record future generations who have gained stewardship of the archive and developed and nurtured it with the care of the above champions, to whom we owe a debt of gratitude!

THE OMNIBUS SOCIETY
SOME HISTORICAL NOTES
The casual reader should note that the Society embraces far more than its archive. At the Society's foundation in late November 1929, the elected Council decided to develop its educational work, as it was then described, in three ways, namely, *by the preparation and reading of papers, by the arrangement of visits, and by the dissemination of information through the medium of its publications*. Many papers were prepared and read on all aspects of bus operation. Talks continue to be given today, but some are more reflective of the career experiences of road passenger transport professionals or illustrations of bus activity using PowerPoint technology.

The *Omnibus Magazine* is the Society's journal of communication. There have been numerous additional publications disseminating information, and much printed material arising from the postal circuits of the earlier years.

Visits to operators and manufacturers' premises have been made throughout the Society's history; especially of note have been those undertaken during annual Presidential Weekends. Members even joined a road test (as guinea-pig passengers) in 1931 (a TSM Express Six, KJ 1612). In June 1958, a nine-day tour of Britain took place, perfectly timed before the advent of motorways. Between 1965 and 1979, continental trips were organised by Brian Chappell or Leslie Nicholson to view transport practices abroad.

Much Society activity is undertaken in its regional branches. Seven members in the Warrington area, led by Cecil Smithies and Jack Baker, put forward a proposal for a North Western Branch, and this started

in 1936. World War 2 prevented any further progress with branch activity, but in 1946, on the demobilisation of Peter Hardy, the branch was restarted and (in 1951) Yorkshire (mooted by Stan Denton in 1946 as a possible separate branch) was formally added to the territory. Recently celebrating its 75th anniversary, a history of the branch was presented in a booklet, well recommended.

In March 1945 George Samson formed a Midland Branch, and during 1946 a healthy number of contacts and visits were made. His early resignation left a gap not filled until March 1947, when H S Stanley took over, 'reinforced' in October of that year by Peter Hardy on his return to Birmingham. A separate branch for South Wales was split off during 1957. In November 1946, John Farthing founded a North East Coast Branch, which became the Northern Branch after Cumberland and Westmorland were 'transferred in' during 1956. Inauguration of the Scottish Branch, promoted by George Train and Jimmie Blair, took place in January 1958. A London & Southern Counties Committee was formed in 1958; lacking branch status, it covered the Channel Islands and overseas as well as much of England south of a line from the Wash to the Severn Estuary. Tony Newman was the first Hon Secretary, its establishment spawning several local groups. It was not until November 1998 that a branch covering the Eastern & Southern parts of England came into being.

The two Research Groups deserve a mention. The London Historical Research Group was formed in March 1963 out of the erstwhile London Bus History Study Group, in which George Robbins had a major involvement. Many senior members of the society were active in the Group

with Reg Westgate taking the leading role. Production of high-quality books and papers has been the hallmark of the intervening years. The Provincial Historical Research Group was founded in 1985 by John Dunabin, to provide the forum for exchange of ideas on research and researching, and has also produced high-quality research publications.

Except for a 19-year period, from 1956 to 1975, branches have generally produced regular reviews or bulletins covering route and vehicle news. Route news continues to thrive, but vehicle news now takes a back seat. However, the Omnibus Society was well into the field of vehicle recording long before the PSV Circle's foundation in 1943. Personal (provincial) fleet recording goes back many years, but it was when Leonard Cox joined in 1936 that the assembly of fleet details from operators all over Britain 'formally' commenced with a team consisting Bernard Phillips and Jimmy La Croix (south), John Parke and John Corner (west), Peter Hardy, Cecil Smithies and Jack Baker (north) and Jimmie Blair and Alan Duke (Scotland). By 1938, they had formulated a remarkably detailed record of national coverage, not achieved by other enthusiast societies until many years later – and long before the advent of Fleet Books. Organised by Traffic Area, the records even then included a registration index, proving invaluable in helping to trace secondhand vehicles. After the 1942 deaths of Messrs Cox, Phillips and Corner, the records were secured by Jimmy La Croix, being developed by him and Charlie Chun to form a unique record. Following discussions, it was mutually agreed to stand down the OS recording scheme as from 1 January 1960 and leave the field to the PSV Circle. The Society continued to produce Fleet Histories jointly with that organisation for many years.

Total membership of the Omnibus Society has long wavered around the 1,000 mark, with the highest year for recruitment being 1950 (when 142 joined), no doubt due to the surge of interest once fellow enthusiasts realised their thirst for knowledge was shared by others. There are still doyen stalwarts whose membership pre-dates that record year.

WHERE TO STOP?
A few approximate figures (see table) to indicate how space for the archive has grown, and continues to grow, by comparing floor areas. Whilst this is only the roughest of measures, its exponential expansion is apparent. The question is, if it continues to grow at the same rate as it has done over the past 70 years, who would provide the resources required to manage it? Time to 'take stock'?

GUIDELINES ON LEGACIES
If you are 'thinning out' your collection, it can be helpful to find out whether you can fill gaps in the collection. To sort material in the approved archive manner would be an added bonus!

Advice was last given on how you could deal with Legacies in OM485 (4-5/09). Some tips were given, as follows:
• Make a will, preferably seeking professional advice.
• Make a clear and specific bequest to the Omnibus Society, quoting our Registered Company Number (3081365), our Charity Number (1048887) and Registered Address (100 Sandwell Street, Walsall, WS1 3EB).
• Tell your partner, friends, relatives and/or executor (preferably all of these!) what you have done and make certain they know what to do when the time comes.
• Mark the items that are the subject of any bequest, so that they are readily identifiable to someone who may not know the difference between waste paper and an historic timetable!
• Let the Society secretary know that a bequest has been made. The address to write to is given above.

COUNCIL ON 28 FEBRUARY 1942
Reading through the annals which show how the persistent OS survived and remained active during the war, the author is struck by the poignancy of the three meetings (AGM; talk by Charles Lee on 'Area Agreements'; inaugural Emergency Committee) all held at The Strand, on the above date, including the agreement to found the Timetable Library, which started it all. Whilst the allies were on their 'back foot', an Emergency Executive Sub-Committee was set up to overlook arrangements for the wartime duration of these dark days in UK history – and so keep the OS alive.

This Council consisted of 14 members. They were: **Charles E Lee, Charles Klapper, E Moffatt, Jack Baker, Bert Chambers, Flight Lieutenant W L Cox, John Gillham, Paul Gomes, F J Grimoldby, Joe Higham, Noel Jackson, Leslie Nicholson, John Parke and Iolo Watkin**.

Of the 14, two would die in the conflict in just a few weeks time, the survivors all serving the OS well – into the 1970s and beyond. We salute you all!

Several members, fighting for the cause, necessarily abandoned their membership, reinstating themselves postwar. As Dave Bubier has pointed out, most of these Edwardian-born gentlemen would have been too young to serve in the Great War, some then being too old to serve in World War 2. Exceptions certainly include F J Grimoldby of Grimsby (what delightful alliteration!) and George Bullock of Sheffield, both born c.1880. This opens up an Aladdin's cave for further study of members born in the Victorian era – generally industry members eg (Orlando Cecil Power, c.1880-1943) whilst the younger ones ran the OS affairs.

1958	Ladbroke Grove at start, three rooms at	9ft x 11ft	**300sq ft**
2006	Coalbrookdale, long warehouse:	715sq ft	
	Coalbrookdale, Wesleyan Chapel	500sq ft	
	Acton	515sq ft	
	Long Eaton, photographic section	270sq ft	**2,000sq ft**
2011	Coalbrookdale, long warehouse	715sq ft	
	Acton	465sq ft	
	Walsall, net of utility rooms		
	- 102 Sandwell Street	900sq ft	
	- 100 Sandwell Street, inc. mezzanine	1,330sq ft	
	Long Eaton, photographic section	590sq ft	**4,000sq ft**

The 2011 figures include some space for expansion.
In addition is the Coalbrookdale Coach House at around 1,500sq ft, which currently stores material not yet possessed by the OS.

By 2030? Too much to handle?   **7,000sq ft?**

HERBERT AND ALBERT REINOHL

Herbert John Reinohl was born in March 1889 in Pimlico, moving to Walham Green two years later, in the same year that the London General Omnibus Company introduced Bell Punch tickets. As a young child, he observed that the horse bus conductors carried bundles of 50 tickets, back to back and held by a broad elastic band. Travelling on the buses with his mother, he soon 'acquired' any bus ticket he could find, but not always successfully as his hand would be slapped if his mother caught him picking up used tickets.

In 1894, his brother Albert was born and when he was old enough, would join in the hobby. Quantity, not quality, governed the early stages of collecting, the aim being to make up bundles of 50 of like-colour, to recreate those in the conductors' boxes, and allow 'playing at buses'.

By the Salisbury Hotel, Fulham, where his father owned the Sherbrooke Dining Room, buses turned or passed through to Fulham Cross or Hammersmith, providing an opportunity to empty the used-ticket boxes, which is where serious collecting began. Relatives and friends were soon trained to pass over many tickets. Tram tickets were collected from both north and south of the Thames. Exchanges were made with other schoolboys who caught the collecting bug. They benefited by learning much about London from the stages printed on the tickets.

Herbert Reinohl left school in 1905, around the time that the motorbus was ascendant, and Vanguard motorbuses appeared on the streets. He soon acquired boxes, allowing the tickets to be preserved in an orderly manner. Tickets from the Provinces were soon added to the collection, mostly by writing to the companies and successfully requesting sets of their tickets.

He was soon researching the origins of the bus in London,

Robert Excell of the London Transport Museum with one of the 180 Reinohl Collection albums held – this depicting a colour sketch of a London Omnibus, the 'City Atlas'. A most varied and comprehensive set, these were largely penned whilst he lived in North America.

and its early history, partly with help from the Science Museum. Clippings from magazines and newspapers followed. From 1907 an interest was taken in the railway companies' involvement in road passenger transport. The brothers spent most of their pocket money in riding buses and trams just to acquire tickets to fill gaps in their collection. They delighted in fares increases as they gave rise to the introduction of new tickets!

Clouds appeared on the horizon in 1914 and, aged 26 and 21, they were mobilised, both seeing active service in France. Sight of former London B and other types allowed moments of relief. After brother Albert lost a leg in 1917, both wondered whether they would survive the war, but they did.

Although the collection survived the duration, interest was temporarily dampened, and there was a shortage of storage space. The decision was taken to keep only one of each kind and the rest were confined to sacks held in the cellar of their mother's home, and then all disposed. In the aftermath of the Great War, there was little thought that anyone else would be interested in these 'duplicates'.

Herbert Reinohl never returned permanently to the UK, continuing to serve in the Army

of Occupation in Germany. Later, he saw service in India, where he made a trip on the Darjeeling railway. September 1923 saw in him in New York where he met up with collectors of 'Transfer Tickets'.

Brother Albert, with the aid of an artificial leg, restored his interest in the collection, this being during the great period of the London Independents.

After a serious discussion on the future of the collection, the brothers decided to assemble a custom-designed series of albums (14in x 12in). They cut sheets to this size, assembled cardboard covers finished in leatherette, and used stamp hinges for loading. Each cover had a different identity.

In 1935, they discussed the future of their massive collection of transport artefacts, formed into 187 albums, contacting the British Museum and the Ministry of Transport. As a result, a future 'Deed of Request' was drawn up and signed on behalf of the Institute of Transport.

War came again and the safety of the collection was feared. Although many new tickets were received, they remained in bundles pending sorting. Even after the war, in 1946, paper for the sleeves was unobtainable.

In a rare visit to the UK, now from Los Angeles where he was then living, Herbert Reinohl gave a talk (from which this note is penned) to the Omnibus Society on 26 November 1954 at the Institute of Transport in Portland Place, London W1, briefly joining the OS at that time (as member 5486). He estimated the number of tickets in the collection to be around 125,000. He declared that the collection was moved to 'this building' – the Institute of Transport that very month.

The collection of 180 albums, defined as the 'Reinohl Collection' now resides in the custody of the London Transport Museum, being held at Acton in the same Museum building as the OS London Archive. Details can be found on www.ltmuseum.co.uk.

OSMART parcels
wrapped and posted
16,225
and counting...

Sale items
advertised by OSMART
150,000
4,864 catalogue pages
152 catalogues

Oldest
regular timetable
(so far)
1895
(in the 'Bath Railway Guide')

TICKETS
FROM 1870 TO DATE
200,000
(fares please!)

Members of the OS since 1929
4,700
(keep heads still – I'll count again!)

Photographic prints & slides
850,000

Photographic negatives
450,000

UK Provincial operators 1912-1974
Time and Fare table books
15,000

UK Provincial operators 1975-2011
Area timetable booklets & map-guides
10,000

UK Local Authorities 1986-2011
Area timetable booklets & map-guides
30,000

London Transport 'Index' Timetable books, 1936-1972
6,000

Standard white boxes assembled
3,177
[staples used = 67,332]

PTE
leaflets
and
map-guides,
1986-2011
Countless!

UK Bus &
Coach operator
leaflets of
all dates and
subjects
Countless!

LARGEST COLLECTIONS BY VOLUME

E Melville Upton
(1962)
40 large crates

Reg Westgate
(2006)
7.5 ton van load

Derek Giles
(2011)
7.5 ton van
350 boxes

....many more
using two
Transit vanloads

 Miles run to retrieve collections... You guess!

WINDMILL

The industrial and Asiatic-property-owned surroundings of Sandwell Street belie a history well worth a browse if you get tired of transport studies! Sandwell Street once formed the road out of Walsall towards West Bromwich, via New Street and Fieldgate, winding its way through the melee of mediaeval and later 'slums' clustered around the parish church of St Matthew. Our premises stand on the crest of a limestone ridge at 514ft., within 6ft. of the highest point. This high land is covered with a thick bed of glacial sand.

Our two premises were built around 1982 on the former back parlours of three houses, numbered 84/86/88 Sandwell Street, once the abodes of families Bradley, Adcock and Miss Beebee. In the 1980s, no.102 Sandwell Street was a metal-working unit, whilst no.100 was 'Windmill Shopfitters'. The later use of both properties was as a 'Design Centre', a name retained on the building. The premises were purchased from the uncle of the author's tree surgeon, whose house overlooks the site from the south. This fine three-storey house is No.1 Doveridge Place, displaying a blue plaque relating to Sir Henry Newbolt (1862-1938), poet and novelist – 'Drake he was a Devon man' and 'Vitai Lampada' – the patriotic 'play up, play up and play the game'. Reality is that Henry lived here for only three years, as a boy! Terraced Nos. 2, 3 and 4 in this row are delightful three-storey retreats still standing after 200 years. There were nos. 5/6, but efforts in 2004 to rebuild them came to nothing.

Facing our property is 'Sandwell Villas', but only one remains. Owners, the Skidmore family, have had businesses in the area for years – look out for the name. The road adjacent to the villas, now Highgate Road, was called Windmill Lane. The area was called 'Windmill', having boasted local windmills since 1305. Look for the remains of an early nineteenth century

sail-less windmill which in turn acted as corn mill, panorama studio with 'camera obscura', astronomical observatory, WW2 observation post, and neglected relic;' a fascinating sight if you can find it – there's an impressive Staffordshire Blue-paved 'snicket' alongside it, between the 'White Lion' and Highgate Road. Further down Highgate Road, look for a 'creepy' 1893 house called 'Cremlin'. Below nearby Drayman Close lies Highgate Brewery, built in 1898 on an old sandpit, but when the well was sunk it dried good sandwells up towards us. Present-day prize brew is 'Highgate Bee-Zone', a delicate golden beer with a nose of honey and a palate of grapefruit! So, the name 'Sandwell Street' relates to itself and not the road to Sandwell,

which was a priory some distance away! To our immediate west lay a forge, now housing. In Bath Road, is St Michael and All Angels' Church (1871) and towards Little London (old name 'Doveridge') is a larger-than-life porticoed former Almshouse, now 77 Bath Road. Most of the buildings mentioned above are Grade II listed and within 400 yards of the Library. Saddlery was the trade carried out in these very streets – by the 1760s patches of metal working trades manufactured harnesses, buckles and spurs. The present 'White Lion' in Sandwell Street, replacing a coaching inn, dates from 1896 and boasts an excellent Edwardian Lounge – and the beer is good! And don't miss viewing a row of town houses at the top of the quaintly named Dandy's Walk.

REFERENCES AND ACKNOWLEDGEMENTS

The sources for the major part of this work have been the OS records, held in Walsall, particularly the Council Minute books, membership lists and *Omnibus Magazines*. It is apparent that there were a few periods, eg 1989-1993, when the OM failed to keep up with the ever-changing locations of the library, and I am deeply indebted to **John Hart** for drawing out the minute detail of movements at this time, demonstrating his thirst for accurate recording. I am grateful to each of the **Editors of the *Omnibus Magazine***, who are listed elsewhere in this publication. The message for future editors is – record it! The accurate recording of Council Minutes is essential, so my appreciation extends to many unnamed **Minute Secretaries**. The Society's 50th and 60th anniversary celebratory publications (*The Golden Omnibus* of 1979 and OM370 of 1989 respectively), proved invaluable, especially for the branch foundations and the John Parke article on early vehicle recording.

Much inspiration has emerged from work on the Walsall inventory. Text of the paper read by Herbert Reinohl in 1954 on a rare visit from Los Angeles focused on 'collecting things', even in the 1890s, and helped to set this phenomenon in true context. I am indebted to **Dave Bubier**, whose previous work in drawing the strings of early OS history has been invaluable, particularly in the run up to 1942, when my opus took off. Significantly, his reconstruction of the early members listing and a letter to him from Iolo Watkin in 1994, describing memories of pre-World War 2 fellow members, such as his colleagues at Index Publishers, is a gem. A shame we have scant photographic identification of most early members. I commend readers to revisit Dave's **'1929 and all that'**, appearing in OM458, describing the background to the creation of the OS.

Chris Warn, who sadly passed away during the drafting of this publication, had allowed me access to the presentation he gave to the Midland Branch in early 2011, his borrowed illustrations lightening my otherwise dry text. His digital presentation remains with the Library in Walsall and can be made available for appropriate occasions on request to the Librarian.

Our neighbour at Walsall, Philip Venables, helped with some of Windmill's history, especially through the loan of a local 1938 Directory. OS Members have responded to my calls for information or photographs, amongst whom have been **John Bennett, Derek Broadhurst, Richard Gadsby, Graham Harper, John Howie, Pat and Helen Lidgett, Alan Oxley, Derek Roy, (the late) Dave Ruddom** and Prof **Peter White**. Others claimed they were too young to remember! My thanks to anyone I've missed. That mine of information, **Alan Mills**, the Librarian & Archivist (my gaffer) 'dug out' many things I had never heard of and has been most helpful in reading my drafts and keeping me on track. I owe my appreciation to **Tony Francis** and **Harry Barker** for their unfailing support. Enduring thanks are due to **Barry Le Jeune**, not only an inspiration for the archive development of the past three decades, but for his enthusiasm in proposing this special 70th anniversary booklet. May it celebrate his 27 years at the helm!

A thousand and more members have been involved in the archive at some time, so I offer my forgiveness for not mentioning others of you who have donated material or volunteered service in building our priceless collection.

An 'audit trail', of sorts, exists, 'Version 1' giving some narrative sources, if ever needed.

An intended offshoot from this work will be a separate listing of obituaries, so that future historians will have faster retrieval of these crucial reflections on the lives of those who have nurtured the Society over the decades.

The work could not have been compiled without the enthusiasm, editing and assembly skills of **Gavin Booth**, to whom I'm most grateful.

Finally, the publication and free distribution to members of this work has been funded by the bequest of **Derrick Selby Giles**. I reflect on how 'Derek's last three years coincided so exactly with my own fortuitous bond between Walsall and Westcliff, leaving with me profound memories of the man and his legacy.

UNITS OF MEASUREMENT

The author, having been Metrication Officer for his company in 1972 and once taught 'Measurement', wished to use metric units in this book. Every space or box measured has been in metric – how else can one contain A4 or A5, which is metric paper? However, I have not come across one fellow OS member who understands the system! I am thus coerced to use the approximate 'feet and inches'. Future archaeologists, make of it what you will!

ABOUT THE AUTHOR

E A S (Ted) Gadsby, CEng, C WEM, b.1936 in Manningham, Bradford. Formatively living by a bus terminus, the low position of his kid's tricycle facilitated recording new khaki utility Daimler CWA6 unladen weights and predicting crew patterns. Five years schooling in Oxford brought unchaperoned rail travel, prizes for maths and sculling, love of dreamy spires and City of Oxford Motor Services. Joining the embryo West Yorkshire Information Service, he conducted for West Yorkshire Road Car company at Bradford, soon being coerced by John Cockshott to edit the WYIS bulletin. Qualifying as a civil engineer, he joined the water supply industry in Sheffield, just in time to commute by tram (old style), and where he met 1932 member George Bullock, little realising that 50 years later the author would acknowledge his pioneer assistance in starting the OS Timetable Library. A 1955 Omnibus Society member, Ted lapsed on moving to Birmingham – career and courting being more important! Birmingham found him working next door to the Birmingham & Midland Motor Omnibus company's Carlyle

Road Works, leading to inevitable distractions. Ted rejoined the OS in 1988, promptly being posted to sub-Saharan Malawi and then Nepal on World Bank projects. On retirement, Ted became Midland Branch Chairman (1998-2008) and assisted Alan Mills at the original Library site at Coalbrookdale, being closely involved in the Library's 2007 removal to Walsall.

Ted gathers notes on 1967 OS President Chaceley Humpidge, coincidentally resident in Bradford, then Sheffield. A lifetime pastime is managing fictional bus (and now trolleybus) operations. Ted's wide interests include maps, railways, townscapes and church architecture. Travelling to the Amazon and reading about the Anglo-Saxons and African exploration are further interests. His passion is studying the development of polyphony and singing newly-restored sacred renaissance music.

Ted is married to Lenice (Cristina), who hails from Brazil, giving Ted another centre of bus interest. Daughter Gabriella is a London-based actress. Brother Richard, an OS member, researches early Scottish manufacturers, bus pioneers and their fleets.